Math 4
God's Purpose for Numbers

Writer
Kevin Swanson (BS, Mechanical Engineering; MDiv.)

Contributors
Elliott Best (BS, Mathematics; MS, Mathematics)
Matthew Craft (BA, Mathematics; BA, Computer Science)

Editors
Tammy Sechrist (BS, Biology)
Annerien Potgieter (BS, Mathematics; MS, Education)
Sam Gallagher (BS, Mathematics; MDiv.)
Valerie Moore (BS, Mathematics)

Generations
PASSING ON THE FAITH

1st Printing, 2026.

Printed in the United States of America.

ISBN: 978-1-968345-10-5

Cover Design: Justin Turley
Interior Design and Typeset: Sarah Lee Craig

Published by:
Generations
PO Box 1398
Elizabeth, CO 80107
Generations.org

For more information on this and other titles from Generations, visit Generations.org or call (888) 389-9080.

Math 4

Answer Key

Chapter 1 – Day 1

1. 9 + 8
2. 9 x 8
3. 303 + 105
4. 303 x 105
5. (5 + 6) + 7 = 11 + 7 = 18
6. 5 + (6 + 7) = 5 + 13 = 18
7. (10 + 20) + 30 = 30 + 30 = 60
8. 10 + (20 + 30) = 10 + 50 = 60
9. (5 x 3) x 2 = 15 x 2 = 30
10. 5 x (3 x 2) = 5 x 6 = 30
11. 2 + 0 = 2
12. 6 x 1 = 6
13. 52,524+ 0 = 52,524
14. 7,456 x 1 = 7,456
15. 123,456,789.1; 1 | 2 | 3 | 4 | 5 | 6 | 7 | 8 | 9 | 1
16. 98,765,432.0; _ | 9 | 8 | 7 | 6 | 5 | 4 | 3 | 2 | 0
17. 9,876,543.2; _ | _ | 9 | 8 | 7 | 6 | 5 | 4 | 3 | 2
18. 100,340.1; _ | _ | _ | 1 | 0 | 0 | 3 | 4 | 0 | 1
19. 987,654,321.0; 9 | 8 | 7 | 6 | 5 | 4 | 3 | 2 | 1 | 0
20. 37 + 45 = 82
21. 39 + 27 = 66
22. 56 + 39 = 95
23. 68 – 39 = 29
24. 53 – 27 = 26
25. 95 – 36 = 59
26. 96 – 60 = The ladder must be at least 36 inches high.
27. 16 + 1 = 17 people, 17 x 2 = 34 pieces of pizza altogether.
28. 75 ÷ 3 = You will need to ride 25 miles each day (or 25 kilometers per day).

Chapter 1 – Day 2

1. >, >
2. >, >
3. >, >
4. <, <
5. >
6. >
7. >
8. <

9 – 16. Answers will vary. Parent-teacher to Check

17. 145 x 2 = 290
18. 256 + 659 = 915
19. 234 x 3 = 702
20. 871 + 119 = 990
21. 256 x 3 = 768
22. 234 + 459 = 693
23. 19 + 24
24. 19 x 24
25. 856 + 2,612
26. 856 x 2,612
27. 30
28. 10
29. 470
30. 120
31. 150
32. 1,100

Chapter 1 – Day 3

a. 53,435 + 12,431 = 65,866; 65,866 – 12,431 = 53,435
b. 24,435 + 33,414 = 57,849; 57,849 – 33,414 = 24,435
c. 76,543 + 12,345 = 88,888; 88,888 – 12,345 = 76,543
d. 388 + 311 = 699, 400 + 300 = 700
e. 675 + 543 = 1,218, 700 + 500 = 1,200
f. 457 + 222 = 679, 500 + 200 = 700
g. 3,456 + 2,143 = 5,599, 3,000 + 2,000 = 5,000
h. 7,577 + 2,323 = 9,900, 8,000 + 2,000 = 10,000
i. 5,772 + 925 = 6,697, 6,000 + 1,000= 7,000

1. 325 + 487 + 119 = 931
2. 262 – 138 = 124
3. 158 + 878 + 459 = 1,495
4. 275 – 159 = 116
5. 324 + 543 + 532 = 1,399
6. 353 – 262 = 91
7. 55 ÷ 5 = 11
8. 39 ÷ 3 = 13
9. 48 ÷ 4 = 12

Speed Test

4 × 7 = 28
4 × 2 = 8
5 × 8 = 40
4 × 5 = 20
7 × 7 = 49
9 × 9 = 81
3 × 4 = 12
6 × 9 = 54
3 × 3 = 9
4 × 9 = 36
3 × 7 = 21
9 × 8 = 72
9 × 6 = 54
2 × 8 = 16
5 × 10 = 50
5 × 7 = 35
8 × 8 = 64
6 × 2 = 12
10 x 5 = 50
5 × 6 = 30
6 × 3 = 18
3 × 2 = 6
5 × 3 = 15
6 × 5 = 30
7 × 3 = 21
10 × 8 = 80
9 × 2 = 18

6 × 7 = 42
7 × 10 = 70
4 × 6 = 24
7 × 4 = 28
8 × 10 = 80
2 × 9 = 18
10 × 7 = 70
8 × 2 = 16
2 × 3 = 6
3 × 5 = 15
5 × 5 = 25
8 × 4 = 32
6 × 10 = 60
3 × 8 = 24
3 × 10 = 30
7 × 8 = 56
7 × 6 = 42
7 × 9 = 63
9 × 7 = 63
9 × 5 = 45
10 × 3 = 30
8 × 6 = 48
8 × 7 = 56

Chapter 1 – Day 4

1. 320 (10s place), 325 (1s place), 324.6 (1/10s place)
2. 10,334,000 (1,000s place), 10,300,000 (100,000s place), 10,000,000 (1,000,000s place)
3. THE LORD IS MY SHEPHERD
4. $900 + $220 + $210 + $100 + $100 + $30 = The family must earn $1,560 each month to cover the expenses.
5. 16 x 8 = 128, 2,280 – 128 = 2,152
6. 110 x 3 = $330
7. $330 + $160 + $200 + $100 + $100 + $200 + $50 = $1,140
8. 479 + 220 = 699, 500 + 200 = 700
9. 824 + 167 = 991, 800 + 200 = 1,000
10. 521 + 365 = 886, 500 + 400 = 900
11. 5,555 + 3,333 = 8,888, 6,000 + 3,000 = 9,000
12. 8,412 + 2,147 = 10,559, 8,000 + 2,000 = 10,000
13. 6,841 + 1,155 = 7,996, 7,000 + 1,000 = 8,000

Chapter 1 – Day 5

a. 2 missing chunks of ten
b. Add 20 blocks to the left side
c. 30 – 10 = 20
d. 93 – 37 = 56, *n* = 56
e. *n* = 56
f. 60 – 40 = 20, *n* = 20
g. 43 – 13 = 30, *n* = 30
h. 62 – 45 = 17, *n* = 17
1. *n* = 2
2. *n* = 5
3. *n* = 8
4. 2, 4, 6, 8, 10, 12, 14, 16
5. 22, 20, 18, 16, 14, 12, 10, 8
6. 30, 27, 24, 21, 18, 15, 12, 9
7. 3, 6, 9, 12, 15, 18, 21, 24
8. Division
9. Addition
10. Subtraction
11. Addition
12. Division
13. Addition
14. Subtraction
15. Multiplication
16. 433 + 487 = 920
17. 678 – 189 = 489
18. 565 + 348 = 913
19. 553 – 195 = 358
20. 546 + 399 = 945
21. 765 – 488 = 277

Chapter 1 – Day 6

1. 90 – 50 = 40, *n* = 40
2. 57 – 14 = 43, *n* = 43
3. 268 – 148 = 120, *n* = 120
4. 95 – 58 = 37, *n* = 37
5. 395 – 225 = 170, *n* = 170
6. 578 – 149 = 429, *n* = 429
7. *n* = 2
8. *n* = 4
9. *n* = 6
10. 8 + *n* – 8 = 16 – 8, *n* = 8
11. 10 x 5 = 50
12. 3 x 12 = 36
13. 4 x 11 = 44
14. 4 x 12 = 48
15. 12 ÷ 3 = 4
16. 60 ÷ 10 = 6
17. 16 ÷ 4 = 4
18. 72 ÷ 8 = 9
19. 134 x 3 = 402
20. 84 ÷ 7 = 12
21. 357 x 3 = 1,071
22. 48 ÷ 4 = 12
23. 245 x 3 = 735
24. 75 ÷ 5 = 15
25. $7.99 + $12.99 = $20.98
26. $21.50 – $9.95 = $11.55
27. $7.99 + $12.99 + $8.00 = $28.98 for hat, t-shirt, and a book, $28.98 – $25.00 = Needs $3.98 more.

Chapter 1 – Day 7

a. 507 – 348 = 159
b. 901 – 419 = 482
c. 600 – 398 = 202

1. 28 – 18 = 10, Unknown = 10
2. 40 – 28 = 12, Unknown = 12
3. 56 – 35 = 21, Unknown = 21
4. 62 – 47 = 15, Unknown = 15
5. 120 – 110 = 10, Unknown = 10
6. 209 – 157 = 52, Unknown = 52
7. 25 – 15 = 10, Need 10 more gallons to fill up the tank
8. 10 x $4 = $40.00 to fill up the tank
9. 52 – 28 = 24, 24 miles left on your bike ride
10. 65 – 37 = 28, 28 more minutes until the cake is ready to take out of the oven
11. 11<14, 15>14, 10<14, 13<14, 12<15

Chapter 1 – Day 8

1. 60 + 60 + 35 + 35 = 190 ft
2. 35 + 35 + 20 + 20 = 110 ft
3. 85 + 85 + 15 + 15 = 200 ft
4. 3/7 + 2/7 = 5/7 
5. 5/9 + 4/9 = 9/9 
6. 11/16 + 4/16 = 15/16 
7. <
8. >
9. <
10. >
11. <
12. <
13. 45,678 + 22,221 = 67,899; 67,899 – 22,221 = 45,678
14. 87,654 + 12,345 = 99,999; 99,999 – 12,345 = 87,654
15. 58,387 + 11,311 = 69,698; 69,698 – 11,311 = 58,387
16. 103 – 59 = 44
17. 507 – 138 = 369
18. 400 – 343 = 57
19. 800 – 521 = 279
20. 18 x 9 = 162
21. 2 x 10 = 20 pounds of potatoes
22. 3/6 + 2/6 = 5/6 → 6/6 – 5/6 = 1/6 of the pie left

Chapter 1 – Day 9

a. 5,431 x 9 = 48,879
b. 6,789 x 9 = 61,101
c. 6,666 x 4 = 26,664
d. 3,421 x 9 = 30,789
e. 12,345 x 5 = 61,725
f. 54,321 x 3 = 162,963

1-3.

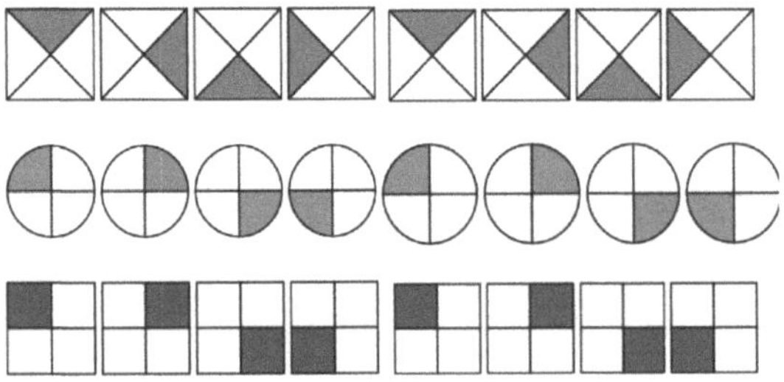

4. 60 – Red
5. 100 – Red
6. 10 – Blue
7. 80 – Red
8. 20 – Blue
9. 40 – Red
10. $n = 2$
11. $n = 2$
12. $n = 7$
13. $n = 11$
14. 1,538 x 3 = 4,614
15. 3,498 x 3 = 10,494
16. 2,459 x 3 = 7,377
17. 35 ÷ 5 = 7
18. 45 ÷ 5 = 9
19. 55 ÷ 5 = 11
20. 65 ÷ 5 = 13

Chapter 1 – Day 10

1. 1" (to nearest inch)
2. 2" (to nearest inch)
3. 4" (to nearest inch)
4. 3" (to nearest inch)
5. 30°
6. 60°
7. 90°
8. 45°
9. <
10. >
11. >
12. >
13. Blue circle, Blue square, Green square
14. Red square, Orange square
15. Orange circle, Green triangle, Orange square
16. Green circle, Pink square, Blue square
17. 264 + 321 = 585; 585 – 321 = 264
18. 875 + 462 = 1,337; 1,337 – 462 = 875
19. 707 – 258 = 449; 449 + 258 = 707
20. $n = 5$
21. $n = 7$
22. $n = 12$
23. $n = 11$

Chapter 1 – Day 11

1. 11 ÷ 3 = 3 R2
2. 9 ÷ 2 = 4 R1
3. 14 ÷ 4 = 3 R2
4. 17 ÷ 4 = 4 R1

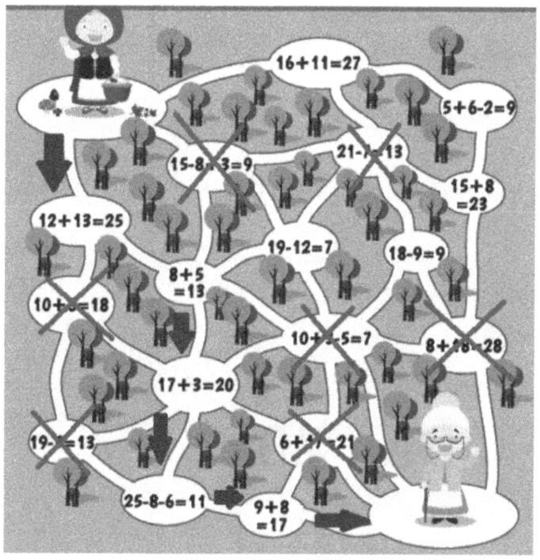

Chapter 1 – Day 12

1. Answers will vary. Student to complete, Parent-teacher to check.
2. Answers will vary. Student to complete, Parent-teacher to check.
3. Answers will vary. Student to complete, Parent-teacher to check.
4. Answers will vary. Student to complete, Parent-teacher to check.
5. Answers will vary. Student to complete, Parent-teacher to check.

Chapter 2 – Day 14

1. 5, 8, 5 x 8 = 40
2. 6, 6, 6 x 6 = 36
3. 7, 9, 7 x 9 = 63
4. 50 – 30 = 20
5. 68 – 28 = 40
6. 53 – 43 = 10
7. 26 – 12 = 14
8. 60 – 25 = 35
9. 60 – 38 = 22
10. 9 ÷ 4 = 2 R1
11. 12 ÷ 5 = 2 R2
12. 22 ÷ 6 = 3 R4
13. 103 – 94 = 9
14. 305 – 136 = 169
15. 100 – 35 = 65
16. 507 – 94 = 413

Chapter 2 – Day 15

a. 90 degrees
b. 180 degrees
c. 270 degrees
d. 360 degrees
e-g.

h. 90°
i. 125°
j. 155°
k. 170°
l. 50°
m. 95°
n. 140°
o. 165°
1-2.

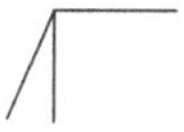

3. 245 – 180 = 65 degrees
4. 270 – 180 = 90 degrees
5. Clock at 4:00 
6. Clock at 5:00 
7. Clock at 6:00 
8. 120 degrees
9. 175 degrees
10. 220 degrees
11. 350 degrees

Chapter 2 – Day 16

1. 490 (10s place), 490 (1s place), 489.6 (1/10s place)
2. 5,000,000 (1,000,000s place), 5,500,000 (100,000s place), 5,498,000 (1,000s place)
3. 1,356 + 3,168 = 4,524, 1,000 + 3,000 = 4,000
4. 4,874 + 2,343 = 7,217
5. 5,000 + 2,000 = 7,000
6. 8,143 + 7,897 = 16,040
7. 8,000 + 8,000 = 16,000
8. 5,432 – 2,345 = 3,087
9. 5,000 – 2,000 = 3,000
10. 9,581 – 3,834 = 5,747
11. 10,000 – 4,000 = 6,000
12. 6,848 – 1,999 = 4,849
13. 7,000 – 2,000 = 5,000
14. 24 ÷ 2 = 12, 50 ÷ 10 = 5
15. 12 ÷ 1 = 12, 30 ÷ 3 = 10
16. 84 ÷ 4 = 21 cars
17. 69 – 38 = 31, unknown = 31
18. 43 – 29 = 14, unknown = 14
19. 170 – 140 = 30, unknown = 30
20. 178 – 119 = 59, unknown = 59

Chapter 2 – Day 17

a. 360° – 30° = 330°
b. 360° – 105° = 255°
c. 360° – 180° = 180°
d. 90°
e. 135°
f. 180°
g. 225°
h. 315°

1. North, 0 degrees
2. Northeast, 45 degrees
3. Southeast, 135 degrees
4. East, 90 degrees
5. Northwest, 315 degrees
6. South, 180 degrees
7. West, 270 degrees

Chapter 2 – Day 18

1.

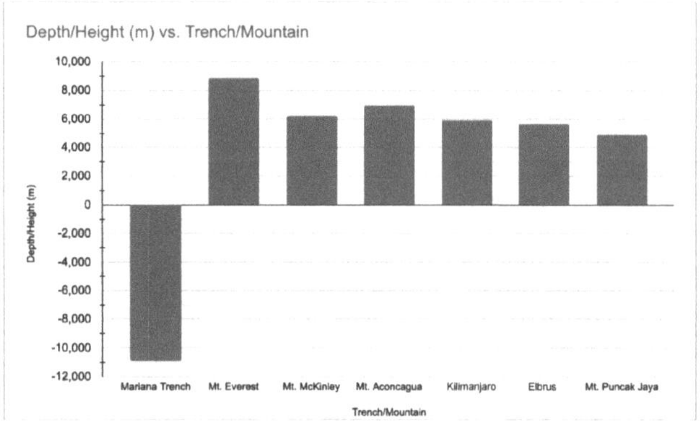

2. 10,935 + 8,850 = 19,785
3. 8,850 – 6,190 = 2,660
4. 6,962 – 6,190 = 772
5. 14 ÷ 5 = 2 R4
6. 10 ÷ 3 = 3 R1
7. 19 ÷ 3 = 6 R1
8. 1/3 
9. 2/3 
10. 6,138 – 2,059 = 4,079, Round 4,000
11. 8,423 – 4,284 = 4,139, Round 4,000
12. 5,619 – 3,457 = 2,162, Round 3,000
13. 9,117 – 1,883 = 7,234, Round 7,000
14. Inside Angle: 130° Outside Angle: 230°
15. Inside Angle: 60° Outside Angle 300°
16. Inside Angle: 90° Outside Angle 270°
17. $n = 6$
18. $n = 2$
19. $n = 7$
20. $n = 15$

Chapter 2 – Day 19

90 – 30 = 60

a. 60 + 30 = 90, Right angle/complementary
b. 55 + 25 = 80, Not a right angle/not complementary
c. 40 + 60 = 100, Not a right angle/not complementary
d. 45 + 45 = 90, Right angle/complementary
e. 15 + 65 = 80, Not a right angle/not complementary
f. 50 + 50 = 100, Not a right angle/not complementary
g. 30 + 50 = 80, Not a right angle/not complementary
h. 75 + 15 = 90, Right Angle/complementary

1. 90 – 13 = 77
2. 90 – 84 = 6
3. 90 – 37 = 53
4. 1,234 x 5 = 6,170
5. 6,475 x 8 = 51,800
6. 5,334 x 5 = 26,670
7. \$134.59 + \$345.55 = \$480.14
8. \$599.00 + \$399.00 = \$998.00
9. \$94.48 + \$166.32 = \$260.80

Chapter 2 – Day 20

1. 80 – 40 = 40
2. 40 – 16 = 24
3. 63 – 25 = 38
4. 3,936 + 7,456 = 11,392
5. 1,359 + 4,777 = 6,136
6. 4,532 + 3,878 = 8,410
7. 2,506 – 399 = 2,107
8. 9,731 – 1,357 = 8,374
9. 5,600 – 3,751 = 1,849
10. 7/4 + 1/4 = 8/4 = 2
11. 18/7 + 9/7 = 27/7
12. 2/4 + 1/4 = 3/4
13. 24/9 + 11/9 = 35/9
14. 360 – 125 = 235
15. 360 – 45 = 315
16. 90 – 55 = 35
17. 90 – 84 = 6
18. \$42 x 4 = \$168
19. \$18 x 4 = \$72
20. \$8 x 9 = \$72
21. \$24 x 3 = \$72
22. \$168 + \$72 + \$72 + \$72 = \$384

Chapter 2 – Day 21

a. 180 – 20 = 160

1. 180 – 145 = 35
2. 180 – 102 = 78
3. 180 – 8 = 172
4. 48 ÷ 3 = 16
5. 55 ÷ 5 = 11
6. 66 ÷ 6 = 11
7. 84 ÷ 7 = 12
8. 1 + 2 + 3 + 4 = 10
9. 3 + 4 + 5 + 6 = 18
10. 6 + 7 + 8 + 9 = 30
11. 7 + 8 + 9 + 10 = 34
12. 2 x 3 x 4 = 24
13. 2 x 4 x 5 = 40
14. 3 x 4 x 3 = 36
15. 5 x 2 x 8 = 80
16. 5 x 3 x 2 = 30

17. (2 + 3) x 3 = 15
18. (1 + 5) x 8 = 48
19. (3 + 4) x 4 = 28
20. $50.00 – $39.87 = $10.13
21. $9.00 x 4 = $36, $50.00 – $36.00 = $14.00 change back
22. 1,100 – 573 = 527 miles left

Chapter 2 – Day 22

1. 180 – 75 = 105, Supplementary
2. 90 – 59 = 31, Complementary
3. 90 – 11 = 79, Complementary
4. 180 – 53 = 127, Supplementary
5. 580 (10s place), 582 (1s place), 581.9 (1/10s place)
6. 12,350,000(1,000s place), 12,300,000 (100,000s place), 12,000,000 (1,000,000s place)
7. 33,251 + 13,633 = 46,884; 46,884 – 13,633 = 33,251
8. 44,383 + 33,416 = 77,799; 77,799 – 33,416 = 44,383
9. 84,735 + 15,244 = 99,979; 99,979 – 15,244 = 84,735
10. 23,243 + 54,443 = 77,686; 77,686 – 54,443 = 23,243
11. $6.00 x 2 = $12.00
12. $4.00 x 4 = $16.00
13. $1.50 x 4 = $6.00
14. $2.00 x 6 = $12.00
15. $12.00 + $16.00 + $6.00 + $12.00 = $46.00
16. $1.50 x 7 = $10.50
17. $3.00 x 4 = $12.00
18. $2.00 x 3 = $6.00
19. $3.00 x 2 = $6.00
20. $10.50 + $12.00 + $6.00 + $6.00 + $4.00 = $38.50
21. ($46.00 – $38.50) The fruit salad will cost more.

Chapter 2 – Day 23

a. 90 + 30 = 120, 180 – 120 = 60
b. 60 + 60 = 120, 180 – 120 = 60
c. 40 + 20 = 60, 180 – 60 = 120
1. _____ + 3 = 5; Unknown = 2
2. 7 + _____ = 9; Unknown = 2
3. _____ – 6 = 2; Unknown = 8
4. 12 – _____ = 3; Unknown = 9
5. _____ x 2 = 8; Unknown = 4
6. 4 x _____ = 12; Unknown = 3
7. _____ ÷ 3 = 5; Unknown = 15
8. 20 ÷ _____ = 4; Unknown = 5
9. 18 ÷ 4 = 4 R2
10. 21 ÷ 4 = 5 R1
11. 26 ÷ 4 = 6 R2
12. 1/2 
13. 1/4 
14. 1,031 x 9 = 9,279
15. 1,321 x 4 = 5,284
16. 2,258 x 4 = 9,032
17. 2,164 x 3 = 6,492
18. 5,433 x 9 = 48,897
19. 6,543 x 9 = 58,887

Chapter 2 – Day 24

1. Answers will vary, Parent-teacher to check
2. Answers will vary, Parent-teacher to check
3. Answers will vary, Parent-teacher to check

Chapter 3 – Day 25

a. 16
b. Day 1 = 80
c. Day 2 = 64
d. Day 3 = 48
e. Day 4 = 32
f. Day 5 = 16
g. 5:30 PM
h. 2:15 PM
i. 12:30 PM
j. Answers will vary
k. 430 – 250 = 180
l. 1870 – 1732 = 138
m. 1155 – 51 = 1,104
1. 12:45 PM
2. 5:15 PM
3. 64 – 38 = 26 ounces left
4. 248 x 9 = 2,232 L
5. 24 + 19 = 43, 96 – 43 = 53 ounces left
6. 3 + 5 = 5 + 3 = 8
7. 12 + 7 = 7 + 12 = 19
8. 7 x 5 = 5 x 7 = 35
9. 4 x 9 = 9 x 4 = 36
10. (2 + 5) + 6 = (5 + 2) + 6 = 13
11. (6 + 2) + 3 = (2 + 6) + 3 = 11
12. (3 x 2) x 5 = (2 x 3) x 5 = 60
13. 5 x (1 x 6) = 5 x (6 x 1) = 30
14. 10 ÷ 3 = 3 R1
15. 14 ÷ 4 = 3 R2
16. 17 ÷ 3 = 5 R2
17. 33 ÷ 3 = 11
18. 44 ÷ 4 = 11
19. 55 ÷ 5 = 11
20. 72 ÷ 6 = 12

Chapter 3 – Day 26

1. 84 ÷ 7 = 12 crackers per day
Sunday = 84
Monday = 72
Tuesday = 60
Wednesday = 48
Thursday = 36
Friday = 24
Saturday = 12
Sunday = 0
2. 70 ÷ 5 = 14 ounces per hour
Start of Hike = 70

Hour 1 = 56
Hour 2 = 42
Hour 3 = 28
Hour 4 = 14
Hour 5 = 0

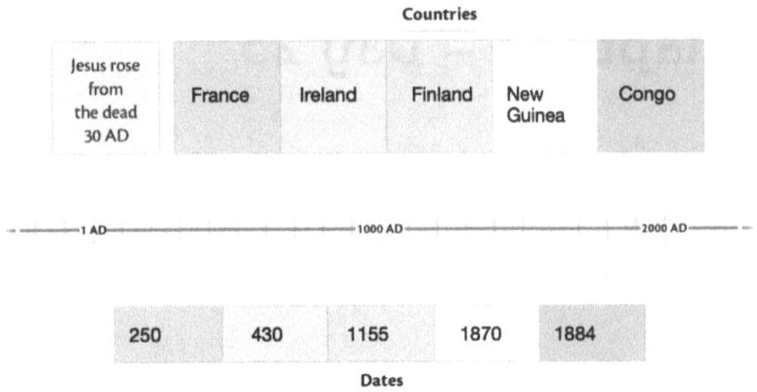

3. 430 – 30 = 400
4. 1155 – 250 = 905
5. 1870 – 430 = 1440
6. 1884 – 1155 = 729
7. 1884 – 30 = 1854
8. 3,244 x 2 = 6,488
9. 5,431 x 8 = 43,448
10. 2,364 x 4 = 9,456
11. 80 ÷ 5 = 16
12. 68 ÷ 4 = 17
13. 22 ÷ 5 = 4 R2
14. n + 3 = 5, 2 +3 = 5
15. n – 6 = 2, 8 – 6 = 2
16. n x 2 = 8, 4 x 2 = 8
17. 20 ÷ n = 4, 20 ÷ 5 = 4
18. 400 – 84 = 316
19. 320 – 58 = 262
20. 505 – 68 = 437
21. 210 – 55 = 155
22. 330 – 288 = 42
23. 402 – 164 = 238

Chapter 3 – Day 27

a. [1, 8)
b. (5, 10)
c. [1, 3]
1. [0, 5) 

2. [2, 7] 

3. [7, 13) 

4. [7, 14] 

5. (0, 59)

6. (10, 31) 

7. 225°
8. 270°
9. 350
10. 290°

11-16.

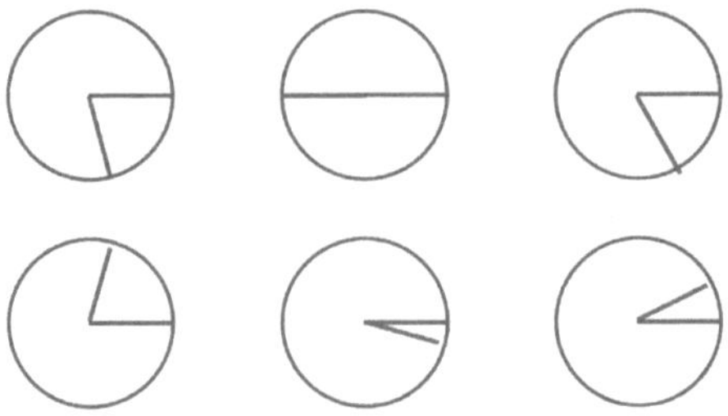

17. 6.45 x 10 = 64.5
18. 12 x 10 = 120
19. 71.3 x 100 = 7130
20. 0.57 x 10 = 5.7
21. 41 x 10 = 410
22. 8.25 x 10 = 82.5
23. 0.34 x 100 = 34.0
24. 63 x 100 = 6300

Chapter 3 – Day 28

1. [7, 10]
2. (7, 10]
3. [4, 8]
4. [6, 24)
5. [1, 30)
6. [1, 30]
7. 83,435 + 12,431 = 95,866; 95,866 – 12,431 = 83,435
8. 24,435 + 33,414 = 57,849; 57,849 – 33,414 = 24,435
9. 76,543 + 12,345 = 88,888; 88,888 – 12,345 = 76,543
10. 56,212 + 32,365 = 88,577; 88,577 – 32,365 = 56,212
11. 42,103 + 18,499 = 60,602; 60,602 – 18,499 = 42,103
12. 0/17
13. 4/17
14. 17/17
15. 0/17
16. 13/17
17. n = 5
18. n = 4
19. n = 7
20. 24 ÷ 3 = 8
21. 42 ÷ 3 = 14
22. 66 ÷ 3 = 22
23. 99 ÷ 3 = 33

Chapter 3 – Day 29

a. 11 (66 ÷ 6)
b. 23 + 8 + 7 + 11 + 16 = 65, 65 ÷ 5 = 13
1. 2 + 4 + 5 + 8 + 6 = 25, 25 ÷ 5 = 5
2. 12 + 15 + 10 + 3 + 20 = 60, 60 ÷ 5 = 12
3. 13°; 90° – 13° = 77°
4. 62°; 90° – 62° = 28°
5. 50°; 90° – 50° = 40°
6. 81°; 90° – 81° = 9°
7. 3,926 x 8 = 31,408

8. 4,717 x 7 = 33,019
9. 9,335 x 6 = 56,010
10. 3,783 x 3 = 11,349
11. 50°; 360° – 50° = 310°
12. 180°; 360° – 180° = 180°
13. 140°; 360° – 140° = 220°
14. 25°; 360° – 25° = 335°
15. 28 ÷ 7 = 4
16. 12 ÷ 6 = 2
17. 20 ÷ 5 = 4
18. 40 ÷ 10 = 4
19. 18 ÷ 3 = 6
20. 8 ÷ 4 = 2
21. 400 – 186 = 214
22. 302 – 145 = 157
23. 812 – 788 = 24
24. 544 – 356 = 188

Chapter 3 – Day 30

1. 308 – 79 = 229
2. 600 – 52 = 548
3. 208 – 129 = 79
4. 15 + 20 + 18 + 12 + 10 = 75 total Bible reading time, 75 ÷ 5 = 15 minutes Bible reading time
5. 9 + 10 + 8 + 11 + 7 = 45, 45 ÷ 5 = 9 pounds average weight of your watermelons, 9 + 11 + 13 + 7 + 10 = 50, 50 ÷ 5 = 10 pounds average weight of friend's watermelons, Friend has larger average watermelon weight by 1 pound more
6. 25 + *n* = 120, 120 – 25 = 95, *n* = 95
7. 18 + *n* = 63, 63 – 18 = 45, *n* = 45
8. 12 + *n*= 49, 49 – 12 = 37, *n* = 37
9. 8 + *n* = 31, 31 – 8 = 23, *n* = 23
10. Perimeter: 5 + 6 + 5 + 6 = 22 cm
11. Perimeter: 12 + 2 + 12 + 2 = 28 cm
12. Perimeter: 4 + 6 + 6 = 16 cm
13. Perimeter: 2 + 7 + 4 +2 + 2 + 5 = 22 cm

Chapter 3 – Day 31

1. 6 x $30 = $180
2. No, $20 short
3. 11 + 8 + 5 = 24, 24 ÷ 3 = 8 bananas eaten on average per week, 11 – 5 = 6 range of bananas per week
4. 25 + 32 + 39 = 96, 96 ÷ 3 = 32 apples eaten on average each month, 39 – 25 = 14 range of apples eaten each month
5. 27 + 42 + 33 = 102, 102 ÷ 3 = 34 potatoes eaten on average per month, 34 x 6 = 204 potatoes eaten in 6 months
6. 5 + 4 + 3 + 6 + 2 = 20, 20 ÷ 5 = 4km average daily walk distance, 6 – 2 = 4 km range, 14 x 4 = 56 km total walking in 14 days
7. 20 + 25 + 18 + 22 + 20 = 105, 105 ÷ 5 = 21, 21 minutes average reading time per evening, 25 – 18 = 7 range, 21 x 10 = 210 minutes read in 10 evenings
8. 59 + 60 + 64 = 183, 183 ÷ 3 = 61 average temperature, 64 – 59 = 5 range

75 + 78 + 81 = 234, 234 ÷ 3 = 78 average temperature, 81 – 75 = 6 range

Denver has more stable temperatures. Dallas is more dependable for warm weather in April.

9. 4 + 9 + 3 + 6 + 8 = 30, 30 ÷ 5 = 6, 6 fish caught on average per day in Lake Michigan, 9 – 3 = 6 fish range. 6 + 6 + 7 + 5 + 6 = 30, 30 ÷ 5 = 6, 6 fish caught on average per day in Lake Tahoe, 7 – 5 = 2 fish range.

Lake Tahoe is more predictable. You could go to either lake and on average at least get 6 fish per day.

10. 7 + 8 + 6 + 7 + 7 = 35, 35 ÷ 5 = 7 hours of sleep on average per night for you, 8 – 6 = 2-hour range. 5 + 10 + 6 + 12 + 7 = 40, 40 ÷ 5 = 8 hours of sleep on average per night for your friend, 12 – 5 = 7-hour range

You have more reliable sleep habits.

Chapter 3 – Day 32

1. 18 + 12 + 17 + 13 + 15 = 75, 75 ÷ 5 = 15 cups of lemonade sold on average each day, 18 – 12 = 6 cup range, 15 x 10 = 150 cups of lemonade sold on average in 10 days.
2. 30 + 25 + 35 + 30 + 25 = 145, 145 ÷ 5 = 29 minutes average practice time per day, 35 – 25 = 10-minute range, 29 x 10 = 290 minutes on average practiced in 10 days.
3. 70 – 25 = 45, *n* = 45
4. 43 – 13 = 30, *n* = 30
5. 45 – 18 = 27, *n* = 27
6. 62 – 55 = 7, *n* = 7
7. 63 – 40 = 23, *n* = 23
8. 20 – 5 = 15, *n* = 15
9. 64 – 28 = 36 ounces is still left in the pitcher
10. 2,000 – 790 = 1,210 ml was drunk
11. 1,400 – 450 = 950 ml cocoa served to your friends
12. 4:00 PM + 1 hour and 45 minutes = 5:45 PM
13. 6:15 PM + 2 hours and 10 minutes = 8:25 PM
14. 350 – 145 = 205
15. 405 – 233 = 172
16. 500 – 324 = 176
17. 605 – 299 = 306
18. 700 – 367 = 333
19. 808 – 496 = 312

Chapter 3 – Day 33

a. 0.4
b. 0.48
c. 0.9
d. 0.90
e. 0.09
f. 3%
g. 4%
h. 39%
i. 8%
j. 76%
k. 40%
l. 0.70 = 70%
m. 0.90 = 90%
n. 0.30 = 30%
o. 0.80 = 80%

p. 0.50 = 50%
q. 0.40 = 40%
1. 1.60 = 160%
2. 2.50 = 250%
3. 1.35 = 135%
4. 1.85 = 185%
5. 2.67 = 267%
6. 3.20 = 320%
7. 102%
8. 195%
9. 123%
10. 249%

Chapter 3 – Day 34

1. 40%
2. 330%
3. 140%
4. 1 2/10, 1.2, 120%
5. 5/100, 0.05, 5%
6. 2 75/100, 2.75, 275%
7. 8/10, 0.8, 80%
8. 2/10, 0.2, 20%
9. South
10. East
11. East
12. Southeast
13. 86%
14. 1.5, 150%
15. 0.40, 40/100
16. 2.25, 2 25/100
17. 100 – 75 = 25%
18. 90 – 42 = 48
19. 90 – 81 = 9
20. 90 – 12 = 78
21. 90 – 39 = 51

Chapter 3 – Day 35

Spreadsheet exercise challenge – Parent-teacher to check
1. 10 ÷ 3 = 3 R1
2. 17 ÷ 2 =8 R1
3. 14 ÷ 3 = 4 R2
4. 20 ÷ 6 = 3 R2
5. 17 ÷ 5 = 3 R2
6. 26 ÷ 5 = 5 R1

Chapter 3 – Day 36

Activities- Parent-teacher to check

Chapter 4 – Day 37

a. 2/100, 0.02, 2%
b. 6/100, 0.06, 6%
c. 15/100, 0.15, 15%
d. 35/100, 0.35, 35%
e. 70/100, 0.70, 70%
f. 9/100, 0.09, 9%
g. 30/100, 0.30, 30%
h. 40/100, 0.40, 40%
i. 7.725 – 2.513 = 5.212
j. 3.338 – 2.116 = 1.222
k. 1.125 – 0.115 = 1.01

l. 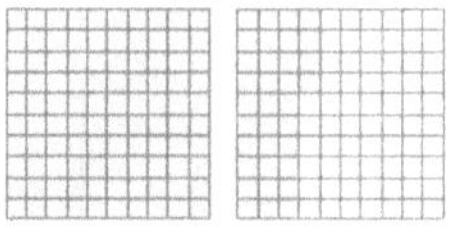

m. 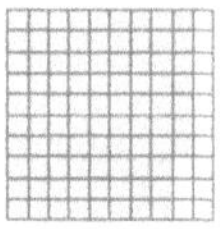

n. 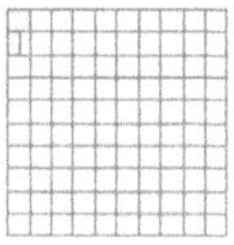

o. 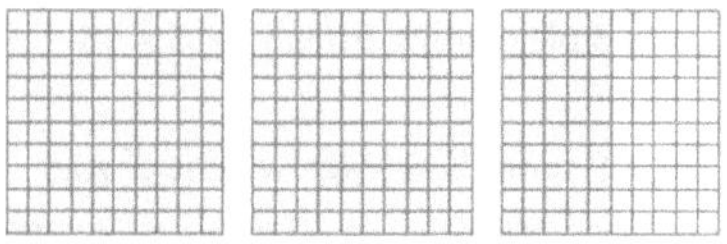

p. 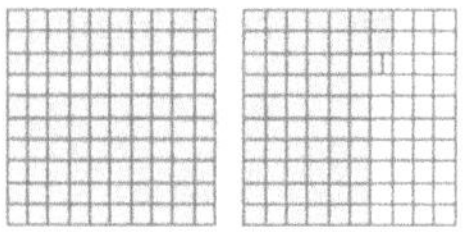

q. 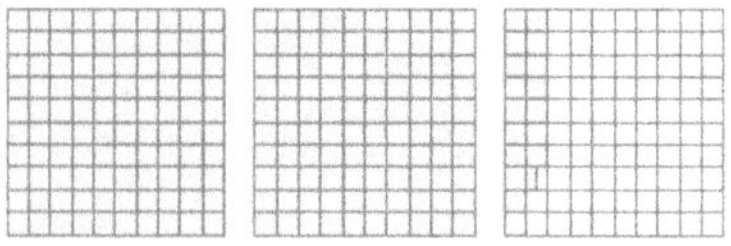

1. 27/100, 0.27, 27%
2. 352/100, 3.52, 352%
3. 781/100, 7.81, 781%
4. 1/100, 0.01, 1%
5. 8/100, 0.08, 8%
6. 850/100, 8.5, 850%
7. 180 – 70 = 110
8. 180 – 127 = 53
9. 180 – 19 = 161
10. 180 – 172 = 8

Chapter 4 – Day 38

1. 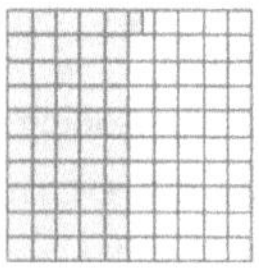

2. 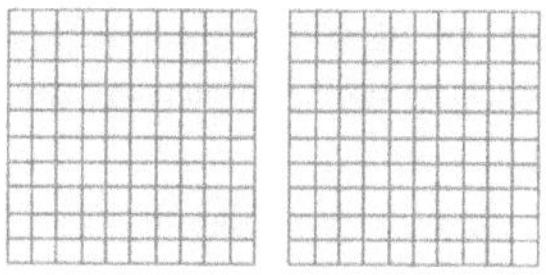

3. 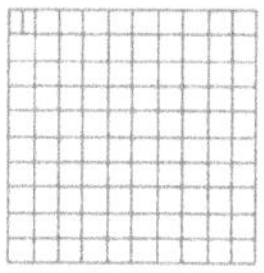

4. 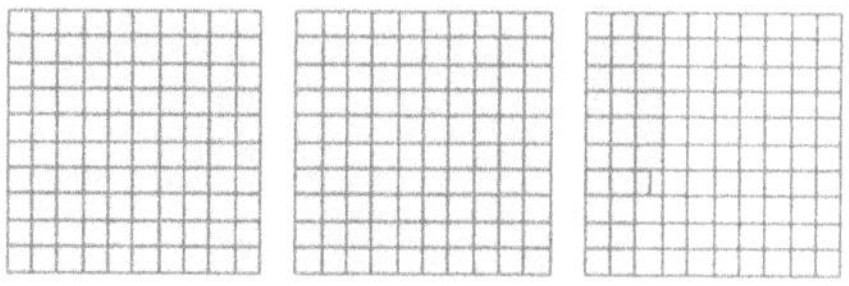

5. 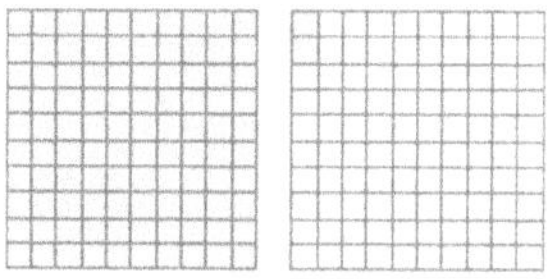

6. 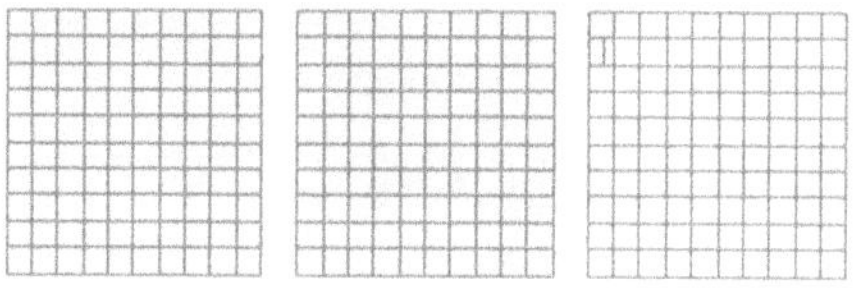

7. 75 + 30 = 105, 180 – 105 = 75 is the missing angle measurement
8. 148 + 15 = 163, 180 – 163 = 17 is the missing angle measurement
9. 120 + 28 = 148, 180 – 148 = 32 is the missing angle measurement
10. 90 + 42 = 132, 180 – 132 = 48 is the missing angle measurement
11. 55 + 35 = 90, 180 – 90 = 90 is the missing angle measurement
12. 40 + 32 = 72, 180 – 72 = 108 is the missing angle measurement
13. >
14. >
15. <
16. >
17. >
18. >
19. 4/6 
20. 2/7 
21. 1/8 
22. 3/4 

Chapter 4 – Day 39

a. 2/4 = 3/6 = 4/8 = 6/12
b. >
c. >
d. <
e. >
f. 2/4 = 4/8  = 
g. 1/2 = 5/10  = 
h. 2/5 = 4/10  = 
i. 1/3 = 2/6 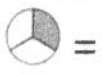 = 
j. 3/5 = 6/10  = 
k. 6/9 = 2/3  = 
l. 1/6 + 2/12 = 1/6 + 1/6 = 2/6
m. 3/6 + 2/8 = 2/4 + 1/4 = 3/4
n. 1/6 + 8/12 = 1/6 + 4/6 = 5/6
1. 6/9 – 1/3 = 2/3 – 1/3 = 1/3
2. 5/6 – 4/12 = 10/12 – 4/12 = 6/12
3. 10/12 – 2/6 = 5/6 – 2/6 = 3/6
4. 5/9 – 1/3 = 5/9 – 3/9 = 2/9
5. 65 ÷ 5 = 13
6. 66 ÷ 6 = 11
7. 66 ÷ 5 = 13 R1
8. 67 ÷ 6 = 11 R1
9. 505 – 349 = 156
10. 905 – 399 = 506
11. 5,830 – 3,342 = 2,488
12. 6,740 – 3,342 = 3,398

Chapter 4 – Day 40

1. 2/12 + 3/6 = 2/12 + 6/12 = 8/12
2. 3/12 + 3/8 = 2/8 + 3/8 = 5/8
3. 5/6 – 2/4 = 5/6 – 3/6 = 2/6
4. 11/12 – 2/8 = 11/12 – 3/12 = 8/12
5. 5/12 + 2/8 = 5/12 + 3/12 = 8/12
6. 3/6 – 6/12 = 3/6 – 3/6 = 0
7. 8.462 – 2.361 = 6.101
8. 7.725 + 1.244 = 8.969
9. 5.987 – 3.456 = 2.531
10. 3.338 + 5.661 = 8.999
11. 1.561 – 1.451 = 0.110
12. 1.125 + 1.452 = 2.577
13. 8 + 3 = 3 + 8 = 11
14. 11 + 4 = 4 + 11 = 15
15. 5 x 3 = 3 x 5 = 15
16. 4 x 8 = 8 x 4 = 32
17. (2 + 4) + 7 = 6 + 7 = 13; 2 + (4 + 7) = 2 + 11 = 13
18. (5 + 1) + 2 = 6 + 2 = 8; 5 + (1 + 2) = 5 + 3 = 8
19. (5 x 2) x 3 = 10 x 3 = 30; 5 x (2 x 3) = 5 x 6 = 30
20. 6 x (2 x 1) = 6 x 2 = 12; (6 x 2) x 1 = 12 x 1 = 12
21. 20 ÷ 3 = 6 R2
22. 40 ÷ 3 = 13 R1
23. 50 ÷ 3 = 16 R2

Chapter 4 – Day 41

a. 1 + 1 + 2 = 4
b. 1/8 + 3/8 = 4/8
c. 4 + 4/8 = 4 4/8
d. 2 1/6 + 3 2/6 + 4 1/6 = 9 4/6
e. 3 2/8 + 4 5/8 = 7 7/8
f. 6 2/100 + 5 5/100 = 11 7/100
1. 2,143 + 1,452 = 3,595; 3,595 – 1,452 = 2,143
2. 5,430 + 1,243 = 6,673; 6,673 – 1,243 = 5,430
3. 6,241 + 2,352 = 8,593; 8,593 – 2,352 = 6,241
4. 4,567 + 2,322 = 6,889; 6,889 – 2,322 = 4,567
5. 4,521 + 1,234 = 5,755; 5,755 – 1,234 = 4,521

6. 5,123 + 1,234 = 6,357; 6,357 – 1,234 = 5,123
7. $n = 7$
8. $n = 14$
9. $n = 4$
10. $n = 6$
11. 8.553 – 5.444 = 3.109
12. 6.666 – 3.557 = 3.109
13. 3.456 – 1.257 = 2.199
14. Answer will vary, parent-teacher to check
15. Answer will vary, parent-teacher to check
16. Answer will vary, parent-teacher to check
17. Answer will vary, parent-teacher to check

Chapter 4 – Day 42

1. 9 4/5
2. 14 1/2
3. 6 1/7
4. 16 4/5
5. 9 1/3
6. 11 1/2
7. 5 + 6 + 7 = 18, 18 ÷ 3 = 6
8. 10 + 20 + 30 = 60, 60 ÷ 3 = 20
9. 6 + 10 + 20 = 36, 36 ÷ 3 = 12
10. 343 x 3 = 1,029
11. 287 x 3 = 861
12. 4,433 x 4 = 17,732
13. 1,873 x 4 = 7,492
14. Red: 270° Blue: 360° – 270° = 90°
15. Red: 190° Blue: 360° – 190° = 170°
16. Red: 225° Blue: 360° – 225° = 135°
17. Red: 315° Blue: 360° – 315° = 45°
18. Red: 350° Blue: 360° – 350° = 10°
19. Red: 180° Blue: 360° – 180° = 180°
20. 46 ÷ 4 = 11 R2
21. 63 ÷ 5 = 12 R3
22. 54 ÷ 4 = 13 R2
23. 76 ÷ 5 = 15 R1
24. 62 ÷ 4 = 15 R2
25. 84 ÷ 5 = 16 R4

Chapter 4 – Day 43

1. 700 – 128 = 572, 699 – 127 = 572
2. 500 – 347 = 153, 499 – 346 = 153
3. 1,000 – 649 = 351, 999 – 648 = 351
4. 1,000 – 535 = 465, 999 – 534 = 465
5. 6 + 8 + 5 + 9 + 7 = 35, 35 ÷ 5 = 7 cups of water on average per day. 9 – 5 = 4 is the range.
6. 46 + 44 + 50 + 47 + 48 = 235, 235 ÷ 5 = 47 seconds on average per day. 50 – 44 = 6 is the range.
7. 8 + 10 + 11 + 13 + 14 + 10 = 66, 66 ÷ 6 = 11 lap counts on average per day. 14 – 8 = 6 is the range.
8. 42 + 40 + 38 + 44 + 41 = 205, 205 ÷ 5 = 41 minutes on average per day. 44 – 38 = 6 is the range.
9. 90 – 42 = 48 is the missing angle measurement, complementary angle.
10. 180 – 41 = 139 is the missing angle measurement, supplementary angle.
11. 90 – 45 = 45 is the missing angle measurement, complementary angle.
12. 180 – 168 = 12 is the missing angle measurement, supplementary angle.
13. 90 – 81 = 9 is the missing angle measurement, complementary angle.
14. 180 – 90 = 90 is the missing angle measurement, supplementary angle.
15. 0.07 = 7%
16. 0.05 = 5%
17. 1.21 = 121%
18. 0.24 = 24%
19. 0.99 = 99%
20. 1.03 = 103%
21. 0.1 = 0.10 = 10%
22. 1.8 = 1.80 = 180%
23. 2.3 = 2.30 = 230%
24. 0.6 = 0.60 = 60%
25. 0.3 = 0.30 = 30%
26. 1.4 = 1.40 = 140%

Chapter 4 – Day 44

1. 2,005 – 179 = 1,826
2. 3,003 – 396 = 2,607
3. 7,007 – 2,999 = 4,008
4. 5,008 – 4,379 = 629
5. 3,000 – 1,228 = 1,772, 2,999 – 1,227 = 1,772
6. 1,000 – 739 = 261, 999 – 738 = 261
7. 1/3 + 2/6 = 2/6 + 2/6 = 4/6 or 1/3 + 1/3 = 2/3
8. 1/2 + 5/8 = 4/8 + 5/8 = 9/8
9. 1/4 + 3/8 = 2/8 + 3/8 = 5/8
10. 1/4 + 3/6 = 1/4 + 2/4 = 3/4
11. 1/8 + 3/6 = 1/8 + 4/8 = 5/8
12. 2/8 + 1/4 = 2/8 + 2/8 = 4/8 or 1/4 + 1/4 = 2/4
13. 5.873 – 4.464 = 1.409
14. 8.435 + 1.376 = 9.811
15. 7.654 – 2.345 = 5.309
16. 6.466 + 4.538 = 11.004
17. 2.583 – .476 = 2.107
18. 2.499 + 7.554 = 10.053
19. NORTH
20. WEST
21. EAST
22. WEST
23. SOUTH
24. SOUTH

Chapter 4 – Day 45

1.

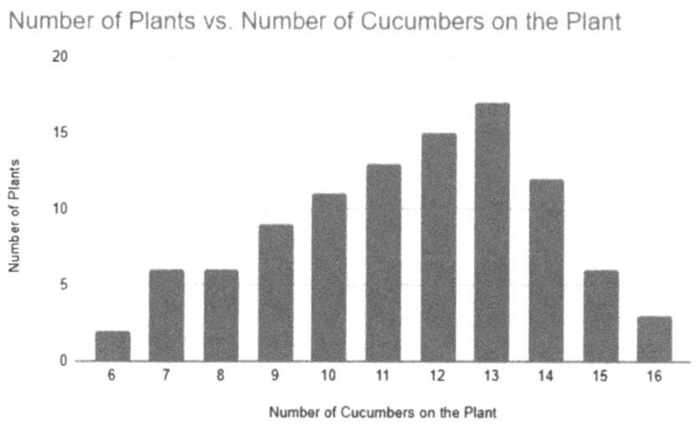

2. Less than 6
3. 16
4. 11, 14 (answers may vary)
5. 13 (answers may vary)
6. 3
7. 7.89 (answers may vary)
8. 1.7
9. No
10. 3
11. 3.97 (answers may vary)
12. 0.7
13. 7/10 = 0.70 = 70%
14. 2
15. 80 (answers may vary)
16. 9
17. 1, 1/10 = 0.10 = 10%
18. 2,316 x 7 = 16,212
19. 8,275 x 5 = 41,375
20. 4,089 x 9 = 36,801
21. 9,637 x 3 = 28,911
22. [8, 10] 
23. [6, 10] 
24. (5, 9) 
25. (4, 9) 
26. (5, 8] 

Chapter 4 – Day 46

1.

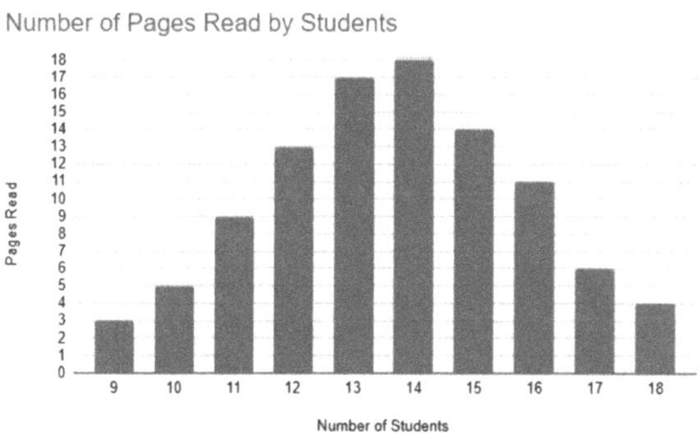

2. 9
3. 18
4. 12, 15 (answers may vary)
5. 14 (answers may vary)
6.

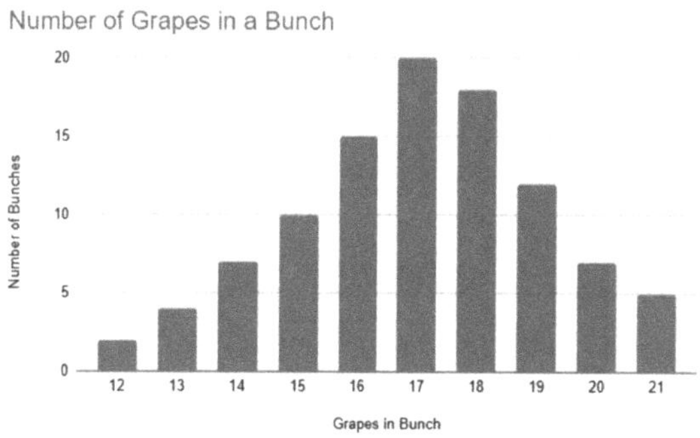

7. 12
8. 21
9. 16, 18 (answers may vary)
10. 17 (answers may vary)
11.

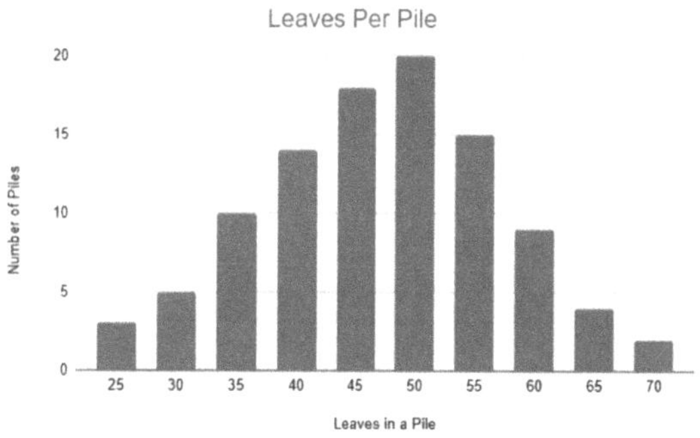

12. 25
13. 70
14. 45, 55 (answers may vary)
15. 50 (answers may vary)
16. EAST
17. NORTH
18. WEST
19. EAST

Chapter 4 – Day 47

a.

b.

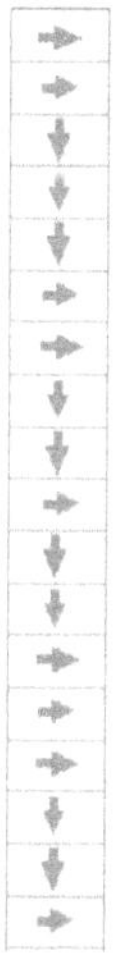

c.

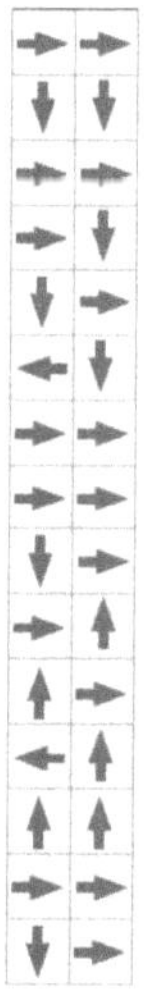

1. 88 ÷ 3 = 29 R1
2. 88 ÷ 4= 11 R0
3. 88 ÷ 5 = 17 R3
4. 88 ÷ 6 = 14 R4
5. 88 ÷ 7 = 12 R4
6. 88 ÷ 8 = 11 R0
7. 3,008 – 2,399 = 609
8. 500 – 399 = 101
9. 9,001 – 8,992 = 9
10. 1,000 – 521 = 479, 999 – 520 = 479
11. 700 – 572 = 128, 699 – 571 = 128
12. 8,000 – 6,192 = 1,808, 7,999 – 6,191 = 1,808
13. 370
14. 8,300
15. 20,500
16. 280
17. 3,700
18. 2,560
19. 5,100
20. 6,000
21. 37
22. 831
23. 2,050
24. 28

Chapter 4 – Day 48

1. Answers will vary, student to complete, parent-teacher to check
2. Answers will vary, student to complete, parent-teacher to check
3. Answers will vary, student to complete, parent-teacher to check
4. Answers will vary, student to complete, parent-teacher to check

Chapter 5 – Day 49

1. 12 x 12 = 144
2. 15 x 11 = 165
3. 14 x 12 = 168
4. 36 x 11 = 396
5. 13 x 11 = 143
6. 21 x 13 = 273
7. 7 2/7 or 6 9/7
8. 10 2/4 or 9 6/4
9. 16 or 14 4/2
10. 6 1/3 or 5 4/3
11. 76 ÷ 5 = 15 R1
12. 87 ÷ 3 = 29 R0
13. 83 ÷ 5 = 16 R3
14. 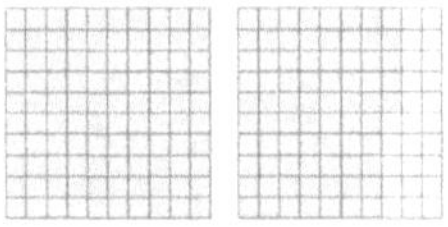
15. 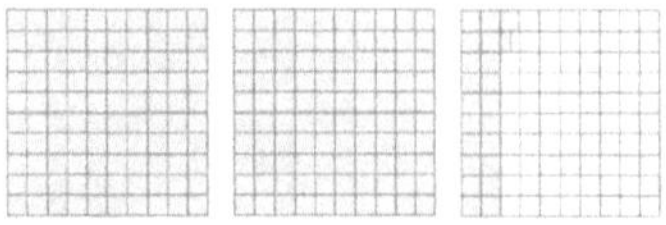
16. 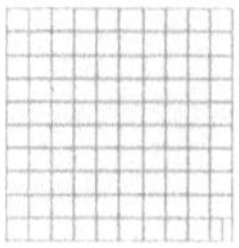
17. 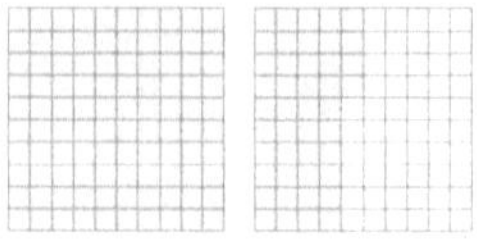
18. 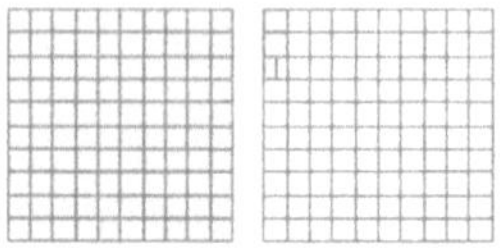
19. 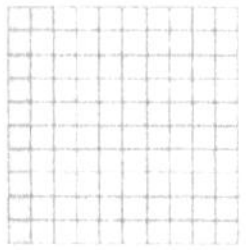
20. [3,8)
21. [1,9]
22. (10,70]
23. [0,20)

Chapter 5 – Day 50

1. 11 x 13 = 143 chairs
2. 14 x 12 = 168 chairs
3. 33 x 12 = 396 chairs
4. 12 x 13 = 156 cookies
5. 50
6. 10
7. 140
8. 600
9. 200
10. 2,010
11. 500
12. 700
13. 100
14. 1,600
15. 2,100
16. 2,000
17. 8 + n = 15, 8 + n – 8 = 15 – 8, n = 7
18. 7 + n= 18, 7 + n – 7 = 18 – 7, n = 11
19. 10 + n = 12, 10 + n – 10 = 12 – 10, n = 2
20. 13 + n = 18, 13 + n – 13 = 18 – 13, n = 5

Speed Drill

1. 4 × 5 = 20
2. 3 × 8 = 24
3. 2 × 3 = 6
4. 7 × 8 = 56
5. 6 × 3 = 18
6. 10 × 2 = 20
7. 8 × 9 = 72

8. 7 × 6 = 42
9. 4 × 8 = 32
10. 2 × 2 = 4
11. 5 × 6 = 30
12. 9 × 6 = 54
13. 3 × 1 = 3
14. 8 × 3 = 24
15. 6 × 4 = 24
16. 3 × 3 = 9
17. 2 × 7 = 14
18. 4 × 0 = 0
19. 3 × 9 = 27
20. 10 × 5 = 50
21. 7 × 3 = 21
22. 5 × 3 = 15
23. 9 × 3 = 27
24. 2 × 4 = 8
25. 4 × 2 = 8
26. 8 × 6 = 48
27. 9 × 2 = 18
28. 2 × 5 = 10
29. 6 × 2 = 12
30. 4 ×10 = 40
31. 8 × 2 = 16
32. 3 × 4 = 12
33. 7 × 5 = 35
34. 10 × 6 = 60
35. 2 × 10 = 20
36. 5 × 7 = 35
37. 6 × 6 = 36
38. 9 × 5 = 45
39. 7 × 4 = 28
40. 8 × 5 = 40
41. 6 × 7 = 42
42. 5 × 4 = 20
43. 9 × 4 = 36
44. 1 × 8 = 8
45. 3 × 9 = 27

Chapter 5 – Day 51

a. 1
b. 3 x 15 = 45
c. 450
1. 30 x 20: 2 zeros, 3 x 2 = 6, 30 x 20 = 600
2. 50 x 200: 3 zeros, 5 x 2 = 10, 50 x 200 = 10,000
3. 30 x 1000: 4 zeros, 3 x 1 = 3, 30 x 1000 = 30,000
4. 7 x 300: 2 zeros, 7 x 3 = 21, 7 x 300 = 2,100
5. 900 x 8,000: 5 zeros, 72, 900 x 8,000 = 7,200,000
6. 600 x 500: 4 zeros, 6 x 5 = 30, 600 x 500 = 300,000
7. 100%
8. 297%
9. 190%
10. 2%
11. 7 5/10, 7.5, 750%
12. 2 7/10, 2.7, 270%
13. 1 2/10, 1.2, 120%
14. 5/100, 0.05, 5%

Speed Drill

1. 20 ÷ 5 = 4
2. 18 ÷ 3 = 6
3. 36 ÷ 6 = 6
4. 27 ÷ 9 = 3
5. 35 ÷ 7 = 5
6. 40 ÷ 8 = 5
7. 30 ÷ 6 = 5
8. 12 ÷ 4 = 3
9. 45 ÷ 5 = 9
10. 24 ÷ 8 = 3
11. 16 ÷ 4 = 4
12. 9 ÷ 3 = 3
13. 25 ÷ 5 = 5
14. 10 ÷ 2 = 5
15. 28 ÷ 7 = 4
16. 63 ÷ 9 = 7
17. 18 ÷ 6 = 3
18. 21 ÷ 3 = 7
19. 42 ÷ 6 = 7
20. 32 ÷ 4 = 8
21. 14 ÷ 2 = 7
22. 36 ÷ 4 = 9
23. 30 ÷ 5 = 6
24. 49 ÷ 7 = 7
25. 16 ÷ 2 = 8
26. 72 ÷ 8 = 9
27. 12 ÷ 3 = 4
28. 18 ÷ 2 = 9
29. 6 ÷ 3 = 2
30. 27 ÷ 3 = 9
31. 48 ÷ 6 = 8
32. 64 ÷ 8 = 8
33. 81 ÷ 9 = 9
34. 56 ÷ 8 = 7
35. 12 ÷ 2 = 6
36. 45 ÷ 9 = 5
37. 8 ÷ 2 = 4
38. 40 ÷ 5 = 8
39. 14 ÷ 7 = 2
40. 16 ÷ 8 = 2
41. 4 ÷ 2 = 2
42. 54 ÷ 9 = 6
43. 9 ÷ 1 = 9
44. 10 ÷ 5 = 2
45. 100 ÷ 10 = 10

Chapter 5 – Day 52

1. 400 x 20 = 8,000 (4 x 2 = 8, + 000 = 8,000)

2. 60 x 20 = 1,200 (6 x 2 = 12 + 00 = 1,200)
3. 7,000 x 4,000 = 28,000,000 (7 x 4 = 28, + 000,000 = 28,000,000)
4. 4,387 x 6 = 26,322
5. 4,520 x 5 = 22,600
6. 82 x 3 = 246
7. 11 x 11 = 121
8. 12 x 14 = 168
9. 11 x 12 = 132
10. 15 x 12 = 180
11. 12 x 13 = 156
12. 18 x 11 = 198
13. <
14. >
15. >
16. <
17. >
18. <
19. 10 + 1 = 11
20. 30 + 3 = 33
21. 70 + 7 = 77
22. 20 + 4 = 24
23. 30 + 6 = 36
24. 60 + 12 = 72

Chapter 5 – Day 53

1. 366 ÷ 6 = 61
2. 357 ÷ 7 = 51
3. 1,266 ÷ 6 = 211
4. 486 ÷ 6 = 81
5. 1,484 ÷ 7 = 212
6. 218 ÷ 7 = 31 R1
7. 3,000 – 728 = 2,272, 2,999 – 727 = 2,272
8. 200 – 129 = 71, 199 – 128 = 71
9. 6,000 – 3,317 = 2,683, 5,999 – 3,316 = 2,683
10. 7,000 – 988 = 6,012, 6,999 – 987 = 6,012
11. 32 x 12 = 384
12. 27 x 11 = 297
13. 14 x 12 = 168
14. 21 x 14 = 294
15. 11 x 15 = 165
16. 24 x 12 = 288
17. 360 – 70 = 290
18. 360 – 220 = 140

Chapter 5 – Day 54

1. 819 ÷ 9 = 91
2. 455 ÷ 5 = 91
3. 168 ÷ 4 = 42
4. 427 ÷ 7 = 61
5. 279 ÷ 3 = 93
6. 186 ÷ 3 = 62
7. 246 ÷ 6 = 41
8. 104 ÷ 2 = 52
9. 11 – 7 = 4
10. 12 – 9 = 3
11. 9 + 10 + 8 + 11 + 7 = 45, 45 ÷ 5 = 9
12. 10 + 9 + 12 + 10 + 9 = 50, 50 ÷ 5 = 10
13. Your friend picked more oranges on average, 1 more orange than you on average
14. 7 – 0 = 7
15. 7 – 2 = 5
16. 4 + 5 + 5 + 7 + 0 + 4 + 3 = 28, 28 ÷ 7 = 4
17. 3 + 7 + 2 + 6 + 3 + 2 + 5 = 28, 28 ÷ 7 = 4
18. 75 + 50 = 125, 180 – 125 = 55
19. 90 + 57 = 147, 180 – 147 = 33
20. 180 – 55 = 125
21. 60 + 60 = 120, 180 – 120 = 60

Chapter 5 – Day 55

a. 800 ÷ 4 = 200 (8 ÷ 4 = 2 + 00 = 200)
b. 2,400 ÷ 6 = 400 (24 ÷ 6 = 4 + 00 = 400)
c. 42,000 ÷ 7 = 6,000 (42 ÷ 7 = 6 + 000 = 6,000)
1. 3,400 ÷ 7: 3,500 ÷ 7 = 500
2. 6,300 ÷ 8: 6,400 ÷ 8 = 800
3. 890 ÷ 11: 890 ÷ 10 = 89
4. 1,500 ÷ 12: 1,500 ÷ 10 = 150
5. 3,950 ÷ 8: 3,950 ÷ 10 = 395
6. 3.670 – 2.862 = 0.808
7. 5.202 – 2.072 = 3.13
8. 1.052 – 0.545 = 0.507
9. 1.890 – 0.925 = 0.965
10. 6.700 – 3.107 = 3.593
11. 5.000 – 2.471 = 2.529
12. 11 ÷ 3 = 3 R2
13. 16 ÷ 5 = 3 R1
14. 23 ÷ 4 = 5 R3
15. 33 ÷ 6 = 5 R3
16. 50 ÷ 7 = 7 R1
17. 1/3 = 2/6 = 3/9 
18. 1/4 = 2/8 = 3/12 

Chapter 5 – Day 56

1. 

2. 900 ÷ 3 → 9 ÷ 3 = 3 → 300
3. 2,400 ÷ 6 → 24 ÷ 6 = 4 → 400
4. 6,400 ÷ 8 → 64 ÷ 8 = 8 → 800
5. 81,000 ÷ 9 → 81 ÷ 9 = 9 → 9,000
6. 150 ÷ 4 → 16 ÷ 4 = 4 → 40
7. 230 ÷ 6 → 24 ÷ 6 = 4 → 40
8. 4,300 ÷ 7 → 42 ÷ 7 = 6 → 600
9. 570 ÷ 8 → 56 ÷ 8 = 7 → 70
10. 7,300 ÷ 9 → 72 ÷ 9 = 8 → 800
11. 10,000 ÷ 3 → 9 ÷ 3 = 3 → 3,000
12. 500 ÷ 9 → 500 ÷ 10 = 50
13. 190 ÷ 8 → 190 ÷ 10 = 19
14. 4,390 ÷ 9 → 4,390 ÷ 10 = 439
15. 59,347 + 34,539 = 93,886; 93,886 – 34,539 = 59,347
16. 34,993 + 11,111 = 46,104; 46,104 – 11,111 = 34,993
17. 24,731 + 43,534 = 68,265; 68,265 – 43,534 = 24,731
18. 48,711 + 44,444 = 93,155; 93,155 – 44,444 = 48,711
19.
   a. 1/8
   b. 3/8
   c. 3/8
   d. 1/8
   e. 4/8
   f. 6/8
   g. 4/8
20. 12 x 12 = 144
21. 144 ÷ 6 = 24
22. $14 x 11 = $154
23. $24 x 12 = $288

Chapter 5 – Day 57

1. THE TREASURE IS GODS WORD
2. F F R F F L F F F
3. F F L F R F F R F F L F
4. F R F L F F L F R F F
5. 427 ÷ 6 = 71 R1
6. 367 ÷ 6 = 61 R1
7. 168 ÷ 8 = 21 R0
8. 489 ÷ 8 = 61 R1
9. 4,500 ÷ 9: 45 ÷ 9 = 5 → 500
10. 270 ÷ 3: 27 ÷ 3 = 9 → 90
11. 32,000 ÷ 4: 32 ÷ 4 = 8 → 8,000
12. 800 ÷ 2: 8 ÷ 2 = 4 → 400
13. 5:45 PM
14. 10:15 AM
15. 11:30 AM
16. 15 + *n* = 63, *n* = 48 (63 – 15 = 48)
17. 63 + *n* = 100, *n* = 37 (100 – 63 = 37)
18. 8/100, 0.08, 8%
19. 17/100, 0.17, 17%
20. 25/100, 0.25, 25%
21. 45/100, 0.45, 45%

Chapter 5 – Day 58

1. F F F R F F R F L F F
2. F R F L F F R F L F F
3.

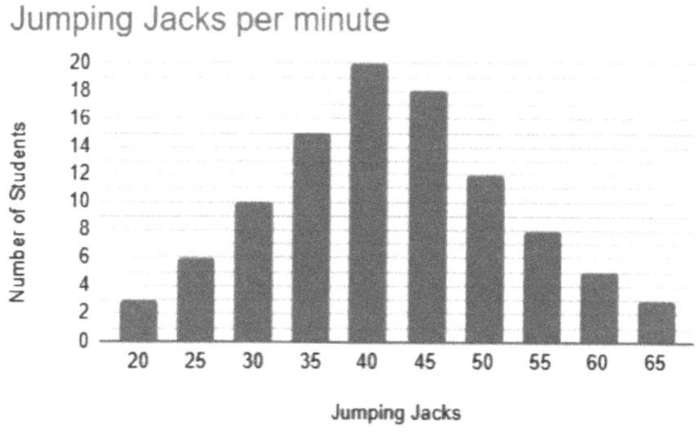

4. 20
5. 65
6. 40 (answers may vary)
7. 81
8.

MINUTES PRACTICED	NUMBER OF STUDENTS
10	4
15	6
20	12
25	14
30	18
35	16
40	12
45	8
50	6
55	4
Total	100

9. 10
10. 55
11. 25, 35 (answers may vary)
12. 30 (answers may vary)
13. 64
14.

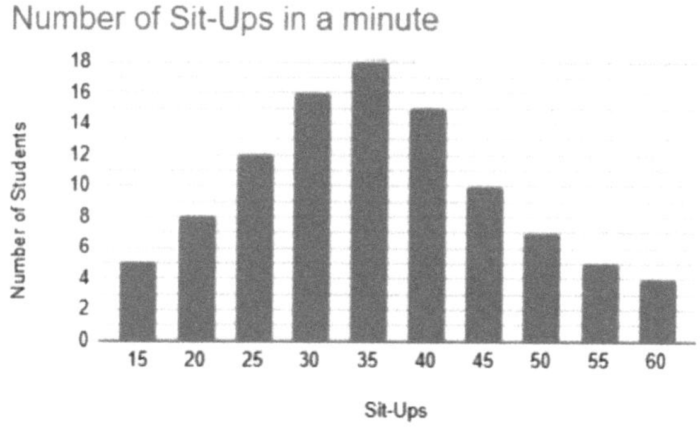

15.

SIT-UPS	NUMBER OF 4TH GRADERS
15	5
20	8
25	12
30	16
35	18
40	15
45	10
50	7
55	5
60	4
Total	100

16. 15
17. 60
18. 30, 40 (answers may vary)
19. 35 (answers may vary)
20. 5
21. 41 x 12 = 492
22. 72 x 11 = 792
23. 31 x 12 = 372
24. 26 x 11 = 286

Chapter 5 – Day 59

a. 430 x 8 = 3,440
b. 430 x 2 = 860
c. 3,440 – 860 = 2,580
d. 1,900 x 6 = 11,400
e. 1,900 x 2 = 3,800
f. 11,400 – 3,800 = 7,600
1. 2,160 ÷ 8 = 270
2. 11 x 13 = 143
3. $7 x 143 = $1,001
4. $3 x 143 = $429
5. $1,001 – $429 = $572
6. 21 x 14 = 294
7. $100 x 294 = $29,400
8. $30 x 294 = $8,820 (3 x 294 = 882)
9. $29,400 – $8,820 = $20,580
10. 2,436 ÷ 6 = 406
11. 4,500 ÷ 5 = 900 (45 ÷ 5 = 9)
12. 3,726 ÷ 6 = 621
13. 5,670 ÷ 7 = 810
14. 1,280 ÷ 8 = 160
15. 1,080 ÷ 9 = 120
16. 270 ÷ 3 = 90 (27 ÷ 3 = 9)
17. 400 x 6 = 2,400 (4 x 6 = 24)
18. 6,300 ÷ 7 = 900 (63 ÷ 7 = 9)
19. 56,000 ÷ 8 = 7,000 (56 ÷ 8 = 7)
20. 300 x 9 = 2,700 (3 x 9 = 27)

Chapter 5 – Day 60

NA –Student to complete with parent-teacher help

Chapter 6 – Day 61

1. 6/8 ÷ 2/2 = 3/4
2. 3/9 ÷ 3/3 = 1/3
3. 6/12 ÷ 3/3 = 2/4
4. 6/12 ÷ 6/6 = 1/2
5. 3/6 ÷ 3/3 = 1/2
6. 22 x 13 = 286
7. 11 x 15 = 165
8. 24 x 12 = 288
9. 81 x 11 = 891
10. 33 x 12 = 396
11. 21 x 14 = 294
12. 2/2 = 2 ÷ 2 = 1
13. 5/5 = 5 ÷ 5 = 1
14. 10/2 = 10 ÷ 2 = 5
15. 40/8 = 40 ÷ 8 = 5
16. 200/2 = 200 ÷ 2 = 100
17. 42,873 + 35,125 = 77,998; 77,998 – 35,125 = 42,873
18. 73,771 + 24,028 = 97,799; 97,799 – 24,028 = 73,771
19. 50,143 + 19,854 = 69,997; 69,997 – 19,854 = 50,143
20. 34,546 + 21,332 = 55,878; 55,878 – 21,332 = 34,546
21. 69,515 – 46,305 = 23,210; 23,210 + 46,305 = 69,515
22. 48,765 – 21,662 = 27,103; 27,103 + 21,662 = 48,765

Chapter 6 – Day 62

1. 2/8 ÷ 2/2 = 1/4
2. 5/10 ÷ 5/5 = 1/2
3. 4/6 ÷ 2/2 = 2/3
4. 3/6 ÷ 3/3 = 1/2
5. 4/10 ÷ 2/2 = 2/5
6. 8/12 ÷ 4/4 = 2/3
7. 420 x 20 = 8,400
8. 6,327 x 9 = 56,943
9. 70 x 70 = 4,900
10. 7,615 x 5 = 38,075
11. 80 x 30 = 8 x 3 = 2,400
12. 6,200 x 40 = 62 x 4 = 248,000
13. 7,000 x 4,000 = 7 x 4 = 28,000,000
14. 82,310 x 300 = 8,231 x 3 = 24,693,000
15. 7:30PM 
16. 3:15PM 
17. 2:15PM 
18. 12:15PM 

19. 2.684 – 1.469 = 1.215
20. 5.431 – 2.162 = 3.269
21. 6.000 – 3.593 = 2.407
22. 17 ÷ 3 = 5 R2
23. 39 ÷ 4 = 9 R3
24. 66 ÷ 9 = 7 R3
25. 2/3 = 4/6 = 6/9 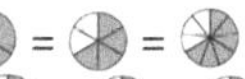
26. 3/4 = 6/8 = 9/12 

Chapter 6 – Day 63

1. 1/5 x 5/10 = 5/50
2. 1/8 x 3/4 = 3/32
3. 7/10 x 5/7 = 35/70
4. 3/5 x 2/9 = 6/45
5. 3/6 x 7/12 = 21/72
6. 255 ÷ 5 = 51
7. 198 ÷ 9 = 22
8. 584 ÷ 8 = 73
9. 453 ÷ 2 = 226 R1
10. 356 ÷ 7 = 50 R6
11. 225 ÷ 6 = 37 R3
12. 4/8 ÷ 2/2 = 2/4
13. 4/8 ÷ 4/4 = 1/2
14. 6/9 ÷ 3/3 = 2/3
15. 7/14 ÷ 7/7 = 1/2
16. 2/10 ÷ 2/2 = 1/5
17. 6/12 ÷ 6/6 = 1/2
18. 1/3 x 1/2 = 1/6
19. 1/4 x 2/3 = 2/12 , 2/12 ÷ 2/2 = 1/6
20. 11 x 1 = 11, 11 x 3 = 33, 11 x 5 = 55, 11 x 9 = 99, 12 x 1 = 12, 12 x 3 = 36, 12 x 5 = 60, 12 x 8 = 96

Chapter 6 – Day 64

1. 1/2 x 1/2 = 1/4
2. 4/5 x 1/4 = 4/20, 4/20 ÷ 4/4 = 1/5
3. 2/3 x 1/6 = 2/18, 2/18 ÷ 2/2 = 1/9
4. 3/5 x 1/3 = 3/15, 3/15 ÷ 3/3 = 1/5
5. 9/12 ÷ 3/3 = 3/4, 3/4 x 1/2 = 3/8
6. 2/3 x 1/4 = 2/12, 2/12 ÷ 2/2 = 1/6
7. 15/20 ÷ 5/5 = 3/4, 3/4 x 1/4 = 3/16
8. 2/3 x 1/2 = 2/6, 2/6 ÷ 2/2 = 1/3
9. 630 ÷ 7 = 90
10. 280 ÷ 4 = 70
11. 120 ÷ 2 = 60
12. 180 ÷ 3 = 60
13. n + 11 – 11 = 15 – 11 → n = 4
14. n + 7 – 7 = 13 – 7 → n= 6
15. 8 + n – 8 = 12 – 8 → n = 4
16. 50 ÷ 8 → 48 ÷ 8 = 6
17. 17 ÷ 3 → 18 ÷ 3 = 6
18. 40 ÷ 6 → 42 ÷ 6 = 7
19. 29 ÷ 5 → 30 ÷ 5 = 6
20. 50 ÷ 10 = 5
21. 800 ÷ 10 = 80
22. 60 ÷ 10 = 6
23. 90 ÷ 10 = 9

Chapter 6 – Day 65

1. 2/3 x 3/3 = 6/9
2. 1/2 x 3/3 = 3/6
3. 1/4 x 2/2 = 2/8
4. 2/5 x 3/3 = 6/15
5. 3/4 x 3/3 = 9/12
6. 3/7 x 2/2 = 6/14
7. 2/8 ÷ 2/2 = 1/4
8. 6/8 ÷ 2/2 = 3/4
9. 5/10 ÷ 5/5 = 1/2
10. 3/12 ÷ 3/3 = 1/4
11. 8/12 ÷ 4/4 = 2/3
12. 3/9 ÷ 3/3 = 1/3
13. 120 – 95 = 25, 95 + 25 = 120
14. 500 – 360 = 140, 360 + 140 = 500
15. 20 – 11 = 9, 11 + 9 = 20
16. 400 – 250 = 150, 250 + 150 = 400
17. 75°
18. 315°
19. 200°
20. 250°
21. 20° 
22. 100° 
23. 195° 
24. 280° 

Chapter 6 – Day 66

1. 12 x 12 = 144, 144 x 4 = 576
2. 576 ÷ 6 = 96
3. 96 x $7 = $672
4. $2,000 – $672 = $1,328
5. 20 x 12 = 240, 20 x 12 = 240, 50 x 12 = 600, 240 + 600 + 240 = 1,080
6. 1,080 ÷ 6 = 180
7. 180 x $4 = $720
8. $2,500 – $720 = $1,780
9. 1/3 x 4/4 = 4/12
10. 1/2 x 6/6 = 6/12
11. 3/5 x 5/5 = 15/25
12. 7/8 x 2/2 = 14/16
13. 7/8 x 3/3 = 21/24
14. 4/9 x 2/2 = 8/18
15. 12/16 ÷ 4/4 = 3/4
16. 6/9 ÷ 3/3 = 2/3
17. 2/10 ÷ 2/2 = 1/5
18. 8/12 ÷ 4/4 = 2/3

19. 3/15 ÷ 3/3 = 1/5
20. 8/14 ÷ 2/2 = 4/7
21. 75 ÷ 2 = 37 R1
22. 94 ÷ 3 = 31 R1
23. 72 ÷ 4 = 18 R0

Chapter 6 – Day 67

a. 3/6 ÷ 3/3 = 1/2
b. 1/3 x 2/2 = 2/6, 1/2 x 3/3 = 3/6, 2/6 + 3/6 = 5/6
c. 2/3 x 2/2 = 4/6, 1/2 x 3/3 = 3/6, 4/6 + 3/6 = 7/6
d. 3/4 x 3/3 = 9/12, 1/3 x 4/4 = 4/12, 9/12 + 4/12 = 13/12
1. 1/2 x 7/7 = 7/14, 3/7 x 2/2 = 6/14, 7/14 + 6/14 = 13/14
2. 3/8 x 4/4 = 12/32, 3/4 x 8/8 = 24/32, 12/32 + 24/32 = 36/32
3. 2/5 x 6/6 = 12/30, 5/6 x 5/5 = 25/30, 12/30 + 25/30 = 37/30
4. Answers may vary
5. 90°
6. 270°
7. Answers may vary
8. 225°
9. 135°
10. Answers may vary
11. 300°
12. 60°
13. Answers may vary
14. 180°
15. 180°
16. Answers may vary
17. 315°
18. 45°
19. Answers may vary
20. 70°
21. 290°

Chapter 6 – Day 68

1. 3/10 x 9/9 = 27/90, 1/9 x 10/10 = 10/90, 27/90 + 10/90 = 37/90
2. 2/3 x 7/7 = 14/21, 4/7 x 3/3 = 12/21, 14/21 + 12/21 = 26/21
3. 8/5 x 4/4 = 32/20, 1/4 x 5/5 = 5/20, 32/20 + 5/20 = 37/20
4. 3/6 x 2/2 = 6/12, 1/2 x 6/6 = 6/12, 6/12 + 6/12 = 12/12
5. 4/5 x 6/6 = 24/30, 1/6 x 5/5 = 5/30, 24/30 + 5/30 = 29/30
6. 3/4 x 9/9 = 27/36, 7/9 x 4/4 = 28/36, 27/36 + 28/36 = 55/36
7. 7.000 – 3.256 = 3.744
8. 5.500 – 2.034 = 3.466
9. 1.002 – 0.341 = 0.661
10. 8.000 – 6.754 = 1.246
11. 2.070 – 1.678 = 0.392
12. 7.382 – 5.431 = 1.951
13. 90 + 37 = 127, 180 – 127 = 53 is the missing angle measurement
14. 40 + 90 = 130, 180 – 130 = 50 is the missing angle measurement
15. 52 + 35 = 87, 180 – 87 = 93 is the missing angle measurement
16. 140 + 21 = 161, 180 – 161 = 19 is the missing angle measurement
17. 60 + 60 = 120, 180 – 120 = 60 is the missing angle measurement
18. 27 + 120 = 147, 180 – 147 = 33 is the missing angle measurement
19. 2/100, 0.02, 2%
20. 20/100, 0.20, 20%
21. 7/100, 0.07, 7%
22. 75/100, 0.75, 75%

Chapter 6 – Day 69

1. (4 x 3) + 1 = 13, 13/3
2. (3 x 5) + 1 = 16, 16/5
3. (2 x 4) + 1 = 9, 9/4
4. (8 x 5) + 2 = 42, 42/5
5. (4 x 2) + 1 = 9, 9/2, 1/2, 1/2 x 9/2 = 9/4
6. (5 x 2) + 1 = 11, 11/2, 4/1, 4/1 x 11/2 = 44/2
7. 18 ÷ 4 = 4 R2
8. 16 ÷ 3 = 5 R1
9. 47 ÷ 5 = 9 R2
10. 39 ÷ 8= 4 R7
11. 88 ÷ 9 = 9 R7
12. 4 + 3 + 3 + 6 + 4 = 20, 20 ÷ 5 = 4 glasses on average
13. 6 – 3 = 3 is the range
14. 10 + 12 + 15 + 11 + 14 + 9 + 13 = 84, 84 ÷ 7 = 12 minutes on average
15. 15 – 9 = 6 is the range
16. 2 + 3 + 3 + 1 + 4 + 5 = 18, 18 ÷ 6 = 3 verses on average
17. 5 – 1 = 4 is the range
18. 45 + 30 + 42 + 53 + 60 = 230, 230 ÷ 5 = 46 minutes on average
19. 60 – 30 = 30 is the range
20. 15 + 14 + 18 + 22 + 21 = 90, 90 ÷ 5 = 18 birds on average
21. 22 – 14 = 8 is the range
22. 2/9 x 3/3 = 6/27
23. 4/10 x 5/5 = 20/50
24. 4/7 x 7/7 = 28/49
25. 9/10 x 3/3 = 27/30

Chapter 6 – Day 70

1. 10/20 ÷ 10/10 = 1/2
2. 6/9 ÷ 3/3 = 2/3
3. 7/21 ÷ 7/7 = 1/3
4. 18/81 ÷ 9/9 = 2/9
5. (2 x 4) + 2 = 10, 2 2/4 = 10/4
6. 10/4 x 1/3 = 10/12
7. 10/12 ÷ 2/2 = 5/6
8. (3 x 4) + 2 = 14, 3 2/4 = 14/4
9. 14/4 x 1/4 = 14/16
10. 14/16 ÷ 2/2 = 7/8
11. (2 x 6) + 4 = 16, 2 4/6 = 16/6
12. 16/6 x 1/3 = 16/18
13. 16/18 ÷ 2/2 = 8/9
14. (3 x 6) + 2 = 20, 3 2/6 = 20/6
15. 20/6 x 1/3 = 20/18
16. 20/18 ÷ 2/2 = 10/9
17. 21 x 17 = 357
18. 71 x 14 = 994
19. 61 x 13 = 793
20. 41 x 15 = 615
21. 91 x 16 = 1,456

22. 31 x 12 = 372

23. 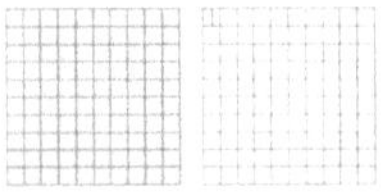

24. 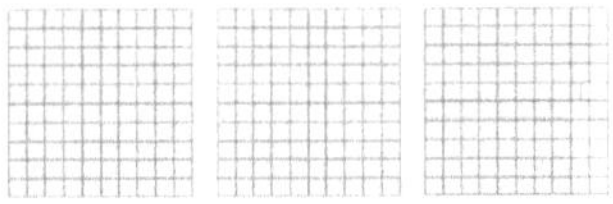

25. 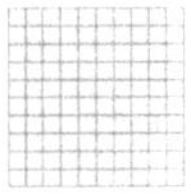

26. 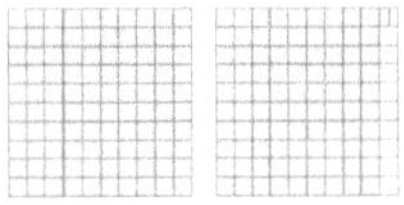

27. 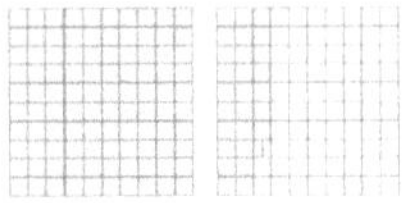

28. 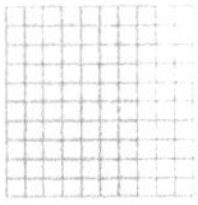

Chapter 6 – Day 71

1. 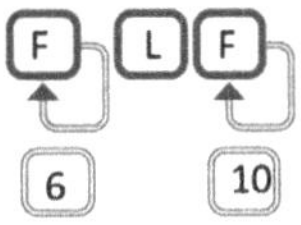

2. 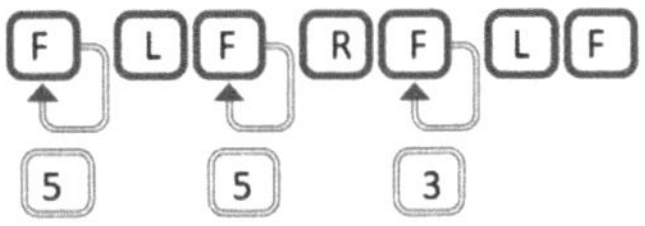

3. F F R F L F F L F F F L F F
4. F F L F F R F F R F F F
5. F F F R F L F F R F F L F F
6.

	A	B
1	Day	**Water Used (liters)**
2	Monday	120
3	Tuesday	135
4	Wednesday	128
5	Thursday	140
6	Friday	125
7	Saturday	150
8	Sunday	138
9	Sum of Weights	=SUM(B2:B8)

7.

	A	B
1	**Dog**	**Weight**
2	Max	42
3	Bella	38
4	Duke	47
5	Spot	44
6	Coco	40
7	Sum of Weights	=SUM(B2:B6)
8	Average	=AVERAGE(B2:B6)
9	Range of Weight	=MAX(B2:B6)–MIN(B2:B6)

8.

	A	B	C	D
1	**Day**	**Tomatoes (lbs)**	**Cucumbers (lbs)**	**Green Beans (lbs)**
2	Monday	60	50	40
3	Tuesday	65	55	45
4	Wednesday	63	53	42
5	Thursday	70	58	47
6	Friday	66	55	44
7	Saturday	72	60	48
8	Sunday	68	57	46
9	Sum of Weights	=SUM(B2:B8)	=SUM(C2:C8)	=SUM(D2:D8)
10	Average	=AVERAGE(B2:B8)	=AVERAGE(C2:C8)	=AVERAGE(D2:D8)
11	Range of Weight	=MAX(B2:B8)-MIN(B2:B8)	=MAX(C2:C8)-MIN(C2:C8)	=MAX(D2:D8)-MIN(D2:D8)

9. 9 68/100, 9.68, 968%
10. 5 3/10, 5.3, 530%
11. 1/1, 1.0, 100%
12. 85/100, 0.85, 85%

Chapter 6 – Day 72

Fraction Activities – Student to complete with parent-teacher

Chapter 7 – Day 73

1. 1, 2, 4, 1 x 4 = 4, 2 x 2 = 4
2. 1, 2, 3, 6, 1 x 6 = 6, 2 x 3 = 6, 3 x 2 = 6
3. 1, 3, 9, 1 x 9 = 9, 2 x _ = 9 (not a whole number), 3 x 3 = 9, 4 x _ = 9 (not a whole number)
4. 1, 2, 7, 14, 1 x 14 = 14, 2 x 7 = 14, 3 x _ = 14 (not a whole number), 4 x _ = 14 (not a whole number), 5 x _ = 14 (not a whole number), 6 x _ = 14 (not a whole number), 7 x 2 = 14
5. 1, 3, 5, 15, 1 x 15 = 15, 2 x _ = 15 (not a whole number, 3 x 5 = 15, 4 x _ = 15 (not a whole number), 5 x 3 = 15, 6 x _ = 15 (not a whole number), 7 x _ = 15 (not a whole number)
6. 1, 2, 3, 6, 9, 18, 1 x 18 = 18, 2 x 9 = 18, 3 x 6 = 18, 4 x _ = 18 (not a whole number), 5 x _ = 18 (not a whole number), 6 x 3 = 18, 7 x _ = 18 (not a whole number), 8 x _ = 18 (not a whole number), 9 x 2 = 18
7. (Left boxes) 1, 2, 3 (Right boxes) 4, 6, 12
8. (Left boxes) 1, 2, 4 (Right boxes) 4, 8, 16
9. (Left boxes) 1, 2, 4, 5 (Right boxes) 8, 10, 20, 40
10. (Left boxes) 1, 3 (Right boxes) 9, 27
11. (Left boxes) 1, 2, 3, 4 (Right boxes) 6, 8, 12, 24
12. 10, 20, 30, 40
13. 4, 8, 12, 16, 20, 24, 28
14. 9, 18, 27, 36, 45
15. 12, 24, 36, 48, 60, 72, 84
16. 32 x 12 = 384
17. 42 x 21 = 882
18. 31 x 15 = 465

19. 51 x 16 = 816
20. 71 x 14 = 994
21. 19 ÷ 2 = 9 R1
22. 82 ÷ 5 = 16 R2
23. 77 ÷ 3 = 25 R2
24. 89 ÷ 7 = 12 R5
25. 22 ÷ 8 = 2 R6

Chapter 7 – Day 74

1. 1, 2, 3, 6, 1 x 6 = 6, 2 x 3 = 6, 3 x 2 = 6
2. 1, 2, 4, 8, 1 x 8 = 8, 2 x 4 = 8, 3 x _ = 8 (none), 4 x 2 = 8
3. 1, 2, 5, 10, 1 x 10 = 10, 2 x 5 = 10, 3 x _ = 10 (none), 4 x _ = 10 (none)
4. 1, 2, 3, 4, 6, 12, 1 x 12 = 12, 2 x 6 = 12, 3 x 4 = 12, 4 x 3 = 12, 5 x _ = 12 (none), 6 x 2 = 12
5. 10/20 ÷ 5/5 = 2/4
6. 24/36 ÷ 6/6 = 4/6
7. 40/100 ÷ 10/10 = 4/10
8. 6/12 ÷ 3/3 = 2/4
9. 8/20 ÷ 2/2 = 4/10
10. 8/64 ÷ 8/8 = 1/8
11. 4,395 x 3 = 13,185
12. 9,245 x 4 = 36,980
13. 6,190 x 5 = 30,950
14. 3,694 x 6 = 22,164
15. 5,312 x 7 = 37,184
16. 8,279 x 8 = 66,232
17. East
18. West
19. South
20. East
21. South
22. West
23. (2 x 2) + 1 = 5 → 5/2
24. (3 x 5) + 3 = 18 → 18/5
25. (4 x 7) + 2 = 30 → 30/7
26. (5 x 9) + 5 = 50 → 50/9

Chapter 7 – Day 75

1	x	60	=	60
2	x	30	=	60
3	x	20	=	60
4	x	15	=	60
5	x	12	=	60
6	x	10	=	60
7	x	~~0~~	=	60
8	x	~~0~~	=	60
9	x	~~0~~	=	60

1. 1 x 24 = 24, 2 x 12 = 24, 3 x 8 = 24, 4 x 6 = 24, 5 x _ = 24 (none), 6 x 4 = 24, 1, 2, 3, 4, 6, 8, 12, 24
2. 1 x 45 = 45, 2 x _ = 45 (none), 3 x 15 = 45, 4 x _ = 45 (none), 5 x 9 = 45, 6 x _ = 45 (none), 1, 3, 5, 9, 15, 45
3. 1 x 72 = 72, 2 x 36 = 72, 3 x 24 = 72, 4 x 18 = 72, 5 x _ = 72 (none), 6 x 12 = 72, 7 x _ = 72 (none), 8 x 9 = 72, 1, 2, 3, 4, 6, 8, 9, 12, 18, 24, 36, 72
4. Composite (9 x 9)
5. Prime
6. Neither
7. Composite (10 x 10)
8. 62 x 24 = 1,488
9. 81 x 34 = 2,754
10. 71 x 33 = 2,343
11. 51 x 52 = 2,652
12. 900 x 70 = 63,000 (9 x 7 = 63)
13. 80 x 300 = 24,000 (8 x 3 = 24)
14. 724 x 20 = 14,480 (724 x 2 = 1,448)
15. 724 x 200 = 144,800 (724 x 2 = 1,448)
16. 724 x 2,000 = 1,448,000 (724 x 2 = 1,448)

17.
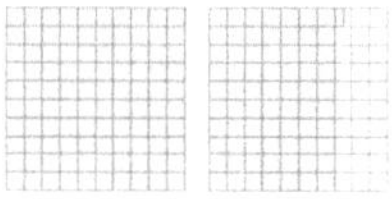

18.
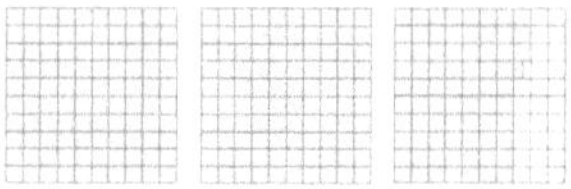

19.
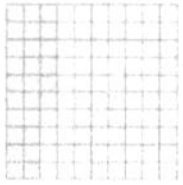

20.
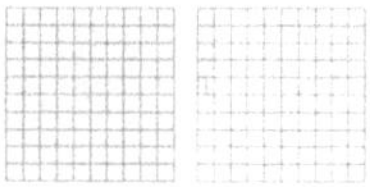

21.
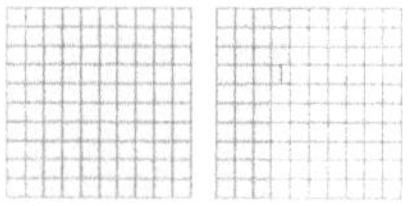

22.
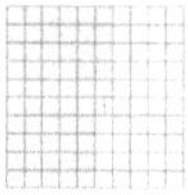

23. 14 x 12 = 168 eggs, $6 x 14 = $84
24. 22 x $4 = $88, 22 x $13 = $286, $286 – $88 = $198 profit
25. 71 x $9 = $639, 71 x $32 = $2,272, $2,272 – $639 = $1,633

Chapter 7 – Day 76

1. 1 x 25 = 25, 5 x 5 = 25, 1, 5, 25
2. 1 x 70 = 70, 2 x 35 = 70, 5 x 14 = 70, 7 x 10 = 70, 1, 2, 5, 7, 10, 14, 35, 70
3. 1 x 28 = 28, 2 x 14 = 28, 4 x 7 = 28, 1, 2, 4, 7, 14, 28
4. 1 x 27 = 27, 3 x 9 = 27, 1, 3, 9, 27
5. 1 x 23 = 23, 1, 23, A Prime Number

6. 1 x 30 = 30, 2 x 15 = 30, 3 x 10 = 30, 5 x 6 = 30, 1, 2, 3, 5, 6, 10, 15, 30
7. 2 2/3 = 6/3 + 2/3 = 8/3
8. 1 2/7 = 7/7 + 2/7 = 9/7
9. 2 1/4 = 8/4 + 1/4 = 9/4
10. 2 3/5 = 10/5 + 3/5 = 13/5
11. 3 1/4 = 12/4 + 1/4 = 13/4
12. 4 2/3 = 12/3 + 2/3 = 14/3
13. (Left boxes) 1, 7 (Right boxes) 7, 49
14. (Left boxes) 1, 2, 3, 4, 6 (Right boxes) 6, 9, 12, 18, 36
15. 305 ÷ 5 = 61
16. 188 ÷ 2 = 94
17. 567 ÷ 7 = 81
18. 75 – 20 = 55, 20 + n = 75, n = 55
19. 14 – 4 = 10, 4 + n = 14, n = 10
20. 58 – 10 = 48, 10 + n = 58, n = 48
21. 48 – 30 = 18, 30 + n = 48, n = 18
22. 23 – 8 = 15, 8 + n = 23, n = 15
23. 60 – 25 = 35, 25 + n = 60, n = 35

Chapter 7 – Day 77

Factors of 8: 1, 2, 4, 8
Factors of 12: 1, 2, 3, 4, 6, 12
Common factors: 1, 2, 4
Greatest common factor: 4
a. 6/12 ÷ 6/6 = 1/2
b. 8/18 ÷ 2/2 = 4/9
c. 8/20 ÷ 4/4 = 2/5
d. 12/36 ÷ 12/12 = 1/3
1. Factors of 9: 1, 3, 9, Factors of 15: 1, 3, 5, 15, GCF: 3
2. Factors of 6: 1, 2, 3, 6, Factors of 18: 1, 2, 3, 6, 9, 18, GCF: 6
3. Factors of 12: 1, 2, 3, 4, 6, 12, Factors of 24: 1, 2, 3, 4, 6, 8, 12, 24, GCF: 12
4. Factors of 21: 1, 3, 7, 21, Factors of 35: 1, 5, 7, 35, GCF: 7
5. Factors of 15: 1, 3, 5, 15, Factors of 25: 1, 5, 25, GCF: 5
6. Factors of 14: 1, 2, 7, 14, Factors of 28: 1, 2, 4, 7, 14, 28, GCF: 14
7. 3/4 x 1/3 = 3/12 (1/4 bag per person)
8. 1/2 x 1/2 = 1/4 bar per person
9. 9/10 x 1/4 = 9/40 bag per person
10. 7/8 x 1/5 = 7/40 per person
11. 5,000 – 921 = 4,999 – 920 = 4,079
12. 700 – 425 = 699 – 424 = 275
13. 1,000 – 819 = 999 – 818 = 181
14. 2,000 – 458 = 1,999 – 457 = 1,542
15. 45 x 51 = 2,295
16. 12 x 63 = 756
17. 72 x 83 = 5,976
18. 32 x 56 = 1,792
19. 12/15
20. 3/15
21. 13/15
22. 0/15
23. 5/15
24. 10/15
25. 12/15
26. 5/15
Extra challenge: Probability that you will pick up a pencil: 10/14, probability that you will pick up a pen: 2/14

Chapter 7 – Day 78

1. Factors of 6: 1, 2, 3, 6, Factors of 12: 1, 2, 3, 4, 6, 12
2. 6/12 ÷ 6/6 = 1/2
3. Factors of 18: 1, 2, 3, 6, 9, 18, Factors of 30: 1, 2, 3, 5, 6, 10, 15, 30
4. 18/30 ÷ 6/6 = 3/5
5. Factors of 20: 1, 2, 4, 5, 10, 20, Factors of 50: 1, 2, 5, 10, 25, 50
6. 20/50 ÷ 10/10 = 2/5
7. Factors of 21: 1, 3, 7, 21, Factors of 35: 1, 5, 7, 35
8. 21/35 ÷ 7/7 = 3/5
9. Factors of 27: 1, 3, 9, 27, Factors of 36: 1, 2, 3, 4, 6, 9, 12, 18, 36
10. 27/36 ÷ 9/9 = 3/4
11. Factors of 8: 1, 2, 4, 8, Factors of 16: 1, 2, 4, 8, 16
12. 8/16 ÷ 8/8 = 1/2
13. 5 + 7 + 6 + 8 + 4 + 6 + 6 = 42, 42 ÷ 7 = 6 glasses of water per day on average
14. 8 – 4 = 4 is the range
15. 6 x 7 = 42, 42 x 12 = 504 glasses of water on average in 12 weeks
16. 25 + 16 + 30 + 20 + 12 + 23 = 126, 126 ÷ 6 = 21 flowers picked per day on average
17. 30 – 12 = 18 is the range
18. 21 x 18 = 378 flowers picked per day in 3 weeks (18 days)
19. 22 + 27 + 16 + 31 = 96, 96 ÷ 4 = 24 acorns collected per day on average
20. 27 – 16 = 11 is the range
21. 31 x 24 = 744 acorns collected in 31 days on average
22. 1/2 x 5/6 = 5/12
23. 1/2 x 5/9 = 5/18
24. 2/3 x 5/7 = 10/21
25. 4/7 x 1/3 = 4/21

Chapter 7 – Day 79

a. 7 rotten bananas, 3 rotten bananas, 3/10 or 30% are good, 7/10 or 70% are rotten.
b. 95 good balloons, 5 popped balloons, 95/100 or 95% are good, 5/100 or 5% are popped.
1. 2/10 or 20% are bad, 8/10 or 80% are good
2. 14/20 or 70% are good, 6/20 or 30% have popped
3. 22/24 or 92% are good, 2/24 or 8% are bad
4. 43/50 or 86% are good, 7/50 or 14% are rotten
5. 5/9 x 5 = 25/45
6. 6/7 x 5 = 30/35
7. 7/10 x 8 = 56/80
8. 8/40 ÷ 8 = 1/5
9. 16/36 ÷ 4 = 4/9
10. 15/27 ÷ 3 = 5/9
11. 170%
12. 50%
13. 197%
14. 220%

15. 9 65/100, 9.65, 965%
16. 1 4/100, 1.04, 104%
17. 4/10, 0.4, 40%
18. 4/100, 0.04, 4%
19. 6.400 – 3.142 = 3.258
20. 7.700 – 1.614 = 6.086
21. 1.200 – 0.741 = 0.459
22. 9.000 – 4.563 = 4.437
23. 3.000 – 2.225 = 0.775
24. 8.300 – 5.931 = 2.369

Chapter 7 – Day 80

1. 13/16 or 81% are good, 3/16 or 19% are burned
2. 15/20 or 75% were bluegill, 5/20 or 25% were largemouth bass
3. 17/50 or 34% were green, 21/50 or 42% were red, 12/50 or 24% were yellow
4. 12/32 or 38% were northern cardinals, 4/32 or 12% were blue jays, 8/32 or 25% were chickadees, and 8/32 or 25% were doves.
5. 4/20 or 20% were daisies, 3/20 or 15% were hydrangeas, 5/20 or 25% were roses, 4/20 or 20% were snapdragons, 4/20 or 20% were zinnias
6. Factors of 10: 1, 2, 5, 10, Factors of 15: 1, 3, 5, 15, GCF: 5
7. 10/15 ÷ 5/5 = 2/3
8. Factors of 9: 1, 3, 9, Factors of 27: 1, 3, 9, 27, GCF: 9
9. 9/27 ÷ 9/9 = 1/3
10. Factors of 7: 1, 7, Factors of 21: 1, 3, 7, 21, GCF: 7
11. 7/21 ÷ 7/7 = 1/3
12. Factors of 8: 1, 2, 4, 8, Factors of 18: 1, 2, 3, 6, 9, 18, GCF: 2
13. 8/18 ÷ 2/2 = 4/9
14. Factors of 4: 1, 2, 4, Factors of 16: 1, 2, 4, 8, 16, GCF: 4
15. 4/16 ÷ 4/4 = 1/4
16. 4 1/4 + 1 1/4 + 2 1/4 = 7 3/4
17. 1 + 2/3 + 3 = 4 2/3
18. 3 1/8 + 1/8 + 1 1/8 + 4 1/8 + 1/8 = 8 5/8
19. 2 2/7 + 4 2/7 = 6 4/7
20. 2 2/13 + 3 2/13 + 5/13 = 5 9/13
21. *n* = 9 (17 – 8)
22. *n* = 13 (18 – 5)
23. *n* = 1 (7 – 6)
24. *n* = 2 (12 – 10)
25. *n* = 5 (30 ÷ 6)
26. *n* = 4 (40 ÷ 10)

Chapter 7 – Day 81

Activity – Child to complete, Parent-teacher to check

1. 1/3 + 1/4 = 7/12; 1/3 x 4/4 = 4/12; 1/4 x 3/3 = 3/12; 4/12 + 3/12 = 7/12
2. 1/4 + 2/5 = 13/20; 1/4 x 5/5 = 5/20; 2/5 x 4/4 = 8/20; 5/20 + 8/20 = 13/20
3. 2/3 + 3/10 = 29/30; 2/3 x 10/10 = 20/30; 3/10 x 3/3 = 9/30; 20/30 + 9/30 = 29/30
4. 8/9 + 1/2 = 25/18; 8/9 x 2/2 = 16/18; 1/2 x 9/9 = 9/18; 16/18 + 9/18 = 25/18
5. 3/5 + 3/4 = 27/20; 3/5 x 4/4 = 12/20; 3/4 x 5/5 = 15/20; 12/20 + 15/20 = 27/20
6. 3/6 + 2/4 = 24/24; 3/6 x 4/4 = 12/24; 2/4 x 6/6 = 12/24; 12/24 + 12/24 = 24/24
7. 22 x 30 = 660
8. 40 x 17 = 680
9. 31 x 27 = 837
10. 61 x 16 = 976
11. 31 x 41 = 1,271
12. 21 x 52 = 1,092
13. 399 ÷ 3 = 133
14. 528 ÷ 6 = 88
15. 512 ÷ 4 = 128
16. 283 ÷ 9 = 31 R4
17. 366 ÷ 7 = 52 R2
18. 443 ÷ 5 = 88 R3
19. 45 x 10 = 450
20. 5.62 x 10 = 56.2
21. 11 x 100 = 1,100
22. 10 x 100 = 1,000
23. 3.54 x 10 = 35.4
24. 12.56 x 100 = 1,256
25. 45.6 x 10 = 456
26. 575 x 10 = 5,750
27. 408.23 x 10 = 4,082.3

Chapter 7 – Day 82

1. Factors of 32: 1 x 32 = 32, 2 x 16 = 32, 4 x 8 = 32, Factors: 1, 2, 4, 8, 16, 32
2. Factors of 41: 1 x 41 = 41, Factors: 1, 41, A prime number is a number with only two factors
3. Factors of 45: 1 x 45 = 45, 3 x 15 = 45, 5 x 9 = 45, Factors: 1, 3, 5, 9, 15, 45
4. Factors of 35: 1 x 35 = 35, 5 x 7 = 35, Factors: 1, 5, 7, 35
5. Factors of 16: 1 x 16 = 16, 2 x 8 = 16, 4 x 4 = 16, Factors: 1, 2, 4, 8, 16
6. Factors of 63: 1 x 63 = 63, 3 x 21 = 63, 7 x 9 = 63, Factors: 1, 3, 7, 9, 21, 63
7. 1 3/4 = (1 x 4) + 3 = 7 = 7/4
8. 2 3/4 = (2 x 4) + 3 = 11 = 11/4
9. 4 5/10 = (4 x 10) + 5 = 45 = 45/10
10. 1 3/17 = (1 x 17) + 3 = 20 = 20/17
11. (7 x 2) + 1 = 15 = 15/2
12. 15/2 x 1/9 = 15/18 liters per bottle
13. 15/18 ÷ 3/3 = 5/6 liters of juice per bottle
14. (10 x 2) + 1 = 21 = 21/2
15. 21/2 x 1/7 = 21/14 pans of lasagna per family
16. 21/14 ÷ 7/7 = 3/2 pans of lasagna per family
17. Multiples of 4: 4, 8, 12, 16, 20
18. Multiples of 5: 5, 10, 15, 20, 25
19. Multiples of 8: 8, 16, 24, 32, 40

Chapter 7 – Day 83

Possible answers for IF-THEN-ELSE statements (answers will vary):

IF: it is snowing, THEN: wear a coat and boots, ELSE: wear lighter clothing

IF: I am hungry, THEN: eat a snack or meal

IF: it is hot outside, THEN: wear a short sleeve shirt, ELSE: wear a long sleeve shirt

F F F IF Gate Open (Arrow up) THEN F ELSE L F F F F

(answers will vary for 1-5)
1. IF: traffic light is green, THEN: go/drive forward, ELSE: stop and wait
2. IF: it is bedtime, THEN: go to bed, ELSE: stay awake
3. IF: sink is full of dishes, THEN: wash the dishes, ELSE: leave the sink alone
4. IF: it is dark outside, THEN: turn on the lights, ELSE: keep the lights off
5. IF: it is raining, THEN: put on a raincoat, ELSE: leave coat at home
6. Factors of 10: 1, 2, 5, 10, Factors of 20: 1, 2, 4, 5, 10, 20, GCF: 10
7. 10/20 ÷ 10 = 1/2
8. Factors of 15: 1, 3, 5, 15, Factors of 25: 1, 5, 25, GCF: 5
9. 15/25 ÷ 5/5 = 3/5
10. Factors of 16: 1, 2, 4, 8, 16, Factors of 24: 1, 2, 3, 4, 6, 8, 12, 24, GCF: 8
11. 16/24 ÷ 8/8 = 2/3
12. Factors of 30: 1, 2, 3, 5, 6, 10, 15, 30, Factors of 45: 1, 3, 5, 9, 15, 45, GCF: 15
13. 30/45 ÷ 15/15 = 2/3
14. 9/24 or 38% are blue, 15/24 or 62% are green
15. 28/40 or 70% are sharpened, 12/40 or 30% are dull
16. 10/27 or 37% are yellow, 9/27 or 33% are orange, 8/27 or 30% are blue
17. 12/28 or 43% are sneakers, 10/28 or 36% are boots, 6/28 or 21% are sandals
18. 9/36 or 25% are carrots, 10/36 or 28% are cucumbers, 8/36 or 22% are peppers, 9/36 or 25% are potatoes
19. 7/21 or 33% are gray, 8/21 or 38% are white, 6/21 or 29% are brown
20. 8/40 or 20% are almonds, 15/40 or 38% are peanuts, 5/40 or 12% are chocolate pieces, 8/40 or 20% are raisins, 4/40 or 10% are cashews
21. 30 x 70 (3 x 7 = 21) = 2,100
22. 40 x 60 (4 x 6) = 2,400
23. 500 x 30 (5 x 3) = 15,000
24. 200 x 800 (2 x 8) = 160,000
25. 40 x 500 (4 x 5) = 20,000
26. 500 x 600 (5 x 6) = 300,000

Chapter 7 – Day 84

1. Student to complete, Parent-teacher to check
2. Student to complete, Parent-teacher to check

Chapter 8 – Day 85

1. 8 x 4 = 32
2. 10 x 4 = 40
3. 12 x 4 = 48
4. 15 x 4 = 60
5. 32 ÷ 4 = 8
6. 40 ÷ 4 = 10
7. 48 ÷ 4 = 12
8. 24 ÷ 4 = 6
9. 68 x 4 = 272
10. 3/9 x 9/9 = 27/81
11. 2/8 x 4/4 = 8/32
12. 5/8 x 8/8 = 40/64
13. 2/15 x 10/10 = 20/150
14. 8/9 x 8/8 = 64/72
15. 7/70 ÷ 7/7 = 1/10
16. 10/90 ÷ 10/10 = 1/9
17. 42/49 ÷ 7/7= 6/7
18. 24/36 ÷ 6/6 = 4/6
19. 1 x 18 = 18, 2 x 9 = 18, 3 x 6 = 18, 3 x 6 = 18, 3 x 3 x 2 = 18
20. 1 x 52 = 52, 2 x 26 = 52, 4 x 13 = 52, 2 x 2 x 13 = 52, 2 x 13 x 2 = 52
21. 1 x 56 = 56, 2 x 28 = 56, 4 x 14 = 56, 7 x 8 = 56, 2 x 2 x 14 = 56, 2 x 2 x 2 x 7 = 56
22. 1 x 75 = 75, 3 x 25 = 75, 5 x 15 = 75, 3 x 25 = 75, 3 x 5 x 5 = 75, 5 x 5 x 3 = 75
23. 1 x 30 = 30, 2 x 15 = 30, 3 x 10 = 30, 5 x 6 = 30, 2 x 3 x 5 = 30, 3 x 5 x 2 = 30
24. 1 x 42 = 42, 2 x 21 = 42, 3 x 14 = 42, 6 x 7 = 42, 2 x 3 x 7 = 42, 2 x 7 x 3 = 42

Chapter 8 – Day 86

1. 22 x 16 = 352
2. 32 x 15 = 480
3. 23 x 16 = 368
4. 38 x 13 = 494
5. 55 x 22 = 1,210
6. 66 x 22 = 1,452
7. 7 x 12 = 84 inches long
8. 5 x 3 = 15 feet wide (3 ft in 1 yd)
9. 12 x 4 = 48 quarts
10. 12 x 16 = 192 ounces
11. 8 x 16 = 128 ounces
12. 4 x 2 = 8 quarts
13. 6/14
14. 14/14
15. 8/14
16. 0/14
17. 9/14
18. 20°, 360° – 20° = 340°
19. 145°, 360° – 145° = 215°
20. 295°, 360° – 295° = 65°
21. 270°, 360° – 270° = 90°

22. 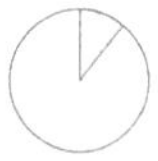

23. 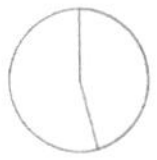

24. 

25. 

Chapter 8 – Day 87

a. 32 x 2.2 = 70.4 pounds
b. 16 x 3.8 = 60.8 liters
c. 12 x 0.6 = 7.2 miles

d. There are 12 inches per 1 foot
e. There are 3 feet in 1 yard.
f. There are 5,280 feet in 1 mile.
g. There are 4 quarts in 1 gallon.
h. There are 128 fluid ounces in 1 gallon.
i. There are 16 ounces in 1 pound.
1. 20 x 12 = 240 inches
2. 15 x 12 = 180 inches
3. 3 x 5,280 = 15,840 feet
4. 3 x 3 = 9 feet
5. 256 ÷ 4 = 64 ounces of water drunk per day
6. 6 x 3 = 18 feet
7. 2 x 16 = 32 ounces
8. 460 ÷ 5 = 92
9. 360 ÷ 6 = 60
10. 490 ÷ 7 = 70
11. 416 ÷ 8 = 52
12. 6 x 2.54 = 15.24 centimeters
13. 4 x 2.2 = 8.8 pounds
14. 5 x 3.8 = 19 liters
15. 5 x 1.6 = 8 kilometers

Chapter 8 – Day 88

1. 42 x 16 = 672 ounces
2. 9 x 16 = 144 ounces
3. 24 x 12 = 288 inches
4. 33 x 12 = 396 inches
5. 9 x 128 = 1,152 ounces
6. 6 x 5,280 = 31,680 feet
7. 3 x 68 = 204 feet
8. 3 x 194 = 582 feet
9. 3 x 515 = 1,545 feet
10. Would need 8 gallons, 8 x 4 = 32 quarts
11. Factors or 6: 1, 2, 3, 6, Factors of 15: 1, 3, 5, 15, GCF: 3
12. Factors of 8: 1, 2, 4, 8, Factors of 18: 1, 2, 3, 6, 9, 18, GCF: 2
13. Factors of 12: 1, 2, 3, 4, 6, 12, Factors of 26: 1, 2, 13, 26, GCF: 2
14. Factors of 15: 1, 3, 5, 15, Factors of 45: 1, 3, 5, 9, 15, 45, GCF: 15
15. (9 + 10) + 13 = 9 + (10 + 13) = 32
16. (4 + 3) + 5 = 4 + (3 + 5) = 12
17. (4 x 3) x 5 = 4 x (3 x 5) = 60
18. 7 x (4 x 1) = (7 x 4) x 1 = 28
19. 90 – 17 = 73, Complementary
20. 180 – 17 = 163, Supplementary
21. 90 – 50 = 40, Complementary
22. 180 – 109 = 71, Supplementary
23. 90 – 63 = 27, Complementary
24. 180 – 151 = 29, Supplementary

Chapter 8 – Day 89

1. 30 x 12 = 360 days
2. 60 x 12 = 720 seconds
3. 50 ÷ 7 = 7 R1
4. 24 x 5 = 120 hours
5. 365 x 50 = 18,250 days
6. 18 ÷ 7 = 2 R4
7. 24 ÷ 3 = 8, 60 x 8 = 480 feedings
8. 30 x 12 = 360 months
9. 60 x 20 = 1,200 seconds
10. 60 x 4 = 240 minutes, 240 x 60 = 14,400 seconds
11. 9 7/8
12. 10 6/7
13. 4 19/24
14. 4 3/4
15. 7 6/14
16. Red: 330° Blue: 360° – 330° = 30°
17. Red: 210° Blue: 360° – 210° = 150°
18. Red: 135° Blue: 360° – 135° = 225°
19. Red: 120° Blue: 360° – 120° = 240°
20. Red: 240° Blue: 360° – 240° = 120
21. Red: 30° Blue: 360° – 30° = 330°

Chapter 8 – Day 90

1. 29 x 11 = 319
2. 99 x 11 = 1,089
3. 84 x 12 = 1,008
4. 91 x 45 = 4,095
5. 45 x 15 = 675 times in 15 minutes
6. 65 ÷ 7 = 9 R2
7. 14 x 30 = 420 hours
8. 15 x 12 = 180 months
9. 124 x 7 = 868 days
10. 34 x 12 = 408 months
11. 9 x 365 = 3,285 days
12. 41 x 7 = 287 days
13. 2 x 52 = 104 weeks
14. West
15. West
16. North
17. West
18. South
19. West
20. Division
21. Addition
22. Subtraction
23. Addition
24. Division
25. Division

Chapter 8 – Day 91

1. 5 x 12 = 60, 60 + 4 = 64 inches
2. 6 x 12 = 72, 72 + 9 = 81 inches
3. 10 x 12 = 120, 120 + 6 = 126 inches
4. 6.40 meters = 640 centimeters
5. 34 kilometers = 34,000 meters
6. 34 x 12 = 408 inches
7. 44 x 12 = 528 inches

8. 29,510 + 17,591 = 47,101; 47,101 – 17,591 = 29,510
9. 52,473 + 43,541 = 96,014; 96,014 – 43,541 = 52,473
10. 44,820 + 15,350 = 60,170; 60,170 – 15,350 = 44,820
11. 34,501 + 37,478 = 71,979; 71,979 – 37,478 = 34,501
12. 65,743 + 24,145 = 89,888; 89,888 – 24,145 = 65,743
13. 71,601 + 14,749 = 86,350; 86,350 – 14,749 = 71,601
14. 115 x 3 = 345 feet
15. 5,280 x 8 = 42,240 feet
16. 3.8 x 4 = 15.2 liters
17. 4 x 16 = 64 ounces
18. 24 x 16 = 384 ounces
19. 2.54 x 7 = 17.78 centimeters
20. 2.2 x 4 = 8.8 pounds
21. Composite
22. Prime
23. Composite
24. Composite
25. Prime
26. Prime

Chapter 8 – Day 92

1. 7 x 12 = 84 inches, 84 + 6 = 90 inches
2. 4 x 12 = 48 inches, 48 + 3 = 51 inches
3. 43 x 12 = 516 inches
4. 56 x 12 = 672 inches
5. 5 x 3 = 15 feet, 15 + 1 = 16 feet
6. 35 x 3 = 105 feet
7. 12.05 x 100 = 1,205 centimeters
8. 15.4 x 1000 = 15,400 meters
9. 8 x 100 = 800 centimeters
10. 14.75 x 1000 = 14,750 meters
11. 14,750 x 100 = 1,475,000 centimeters
12. 6/24 or 25% are chocolate chip cookies, 18/24 or 75% are sugar cookies
13. 8/20 or 40% are monarchs, 7/20 or 35% are swallowtails, 5/20 or 25% are hairstreaks
14. 12/30 or 40% are oaks, 10/30 or 33% are maples, 8/30 or 27% are pines
15. 20/60 or 33% are green, 16/60 or 27% are red, 14/60 or 23% are yellow, 10/60 or 17% are orange
16. 80/100 or 80% sprouted, 20/100 or 20% not sprouted
17. 5/15 or 33% are gray, 10/15 or 67% are brown
18. 1/2 + 3/4 , 1/2 x 4/4 = 4/8, 3/4 x 2/2 = 6/8, 4/8 + 6/8 = 10/8 = 1 1/4
19. 3/4 + 3/8 , 3/4 x 8/8= 24/32, 3/8 x 4/4 = 12/32, 24/32 + 12/32 = 36/32 = 1 1/8
20. 1/3 + 3/12 , 1/3 x 12/12 = 12/36, 3/12 x 3/3 = 9/36, 12/36 + 9/36 = 21/36 = 7/12
21. 18, 20, 22, 24, 26, 28, 30, 32
22. 12, 15, 18, 21, 24, 27, 30, 33
23. 0, 6, 12, 18, 24, 30, 36, 42
24. 54, 48, 42, 36, 30, 24, 18, 12

Chapter 8 – Day 93

a. $20 x 400 = $8,000
b. $50,000 x 10,000 = $500,000,000
c. $4 x 100 = $400
d. The servant had been forgiven a very large debt by the king but refused to forgive a fellow servant who owed him a much smaller debt. The king expected him to show the same compassion he had been shown.
e. He should forgive them and show mercy, just as God forgave him.
f. $960 x 10 = $9,600
g. $960 x 5 = $4,800

1. Answers will vary: a can of soup, a small pineapple, a pair of shoes
2. Answers will vary: a gallon of water, a small dog, a bowling ball
3. Answers will vary: a large bag of dog food, a small bale of hay, a big suitcase when packed
4. Answers will vary: a large adult dog, a washing machine, a heavy wooden desk
5. 23 x 14 = 322
6. 27 x 13 = 351
7. 22 x 19 = 418
8. 15 x 15 = 225
9. 54 x 29 = 1,566
10. 14 x 27 = 378
11. 3/5 + 2/5 = 5/5
12. 3/8 + 2/8 = 5/8
13. 7/5 – 2/5 = 5/5
14. 8/4 – 4/4 = 4/4
15. 3/7 + 4/7 = 7/7
16. 3/4 – 1/4 = 2/4
17. 1/2 + 2/6 = 3/6 + 2/6 = 5/6
18. 3/4 + 1/2 = 3/4 + 2/4 = 5/4

Chapter 8 – Day 94

1. 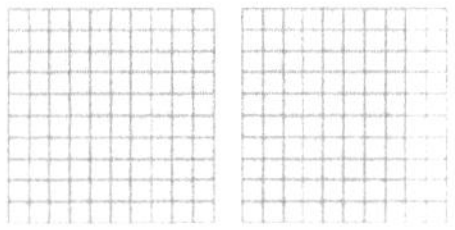

2. 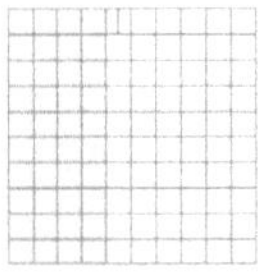

3. 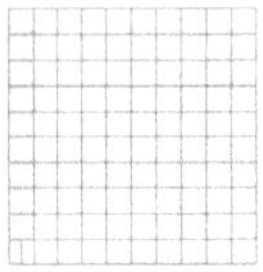

4. 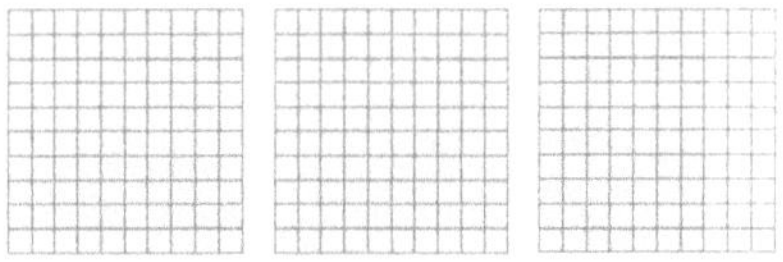

5. 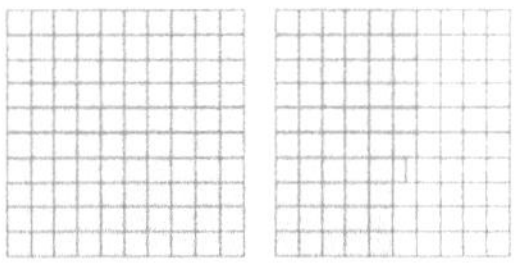

6. 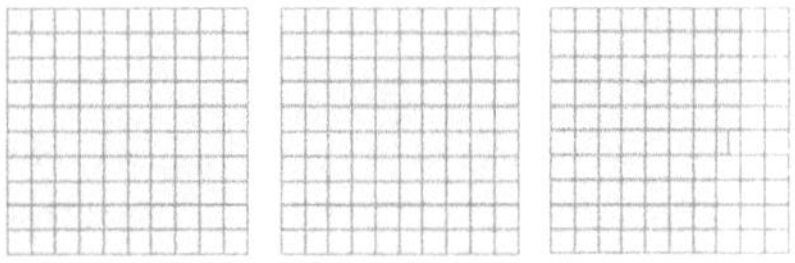

7. 8.836 – 3.927 = 4.909
8. 4.578 – 2.680 = 1.898
9. 2.625 – 0.509 = 2.116
10. 5.725 – 2.188 = 3.537
11. 6.728 – 6.289 = 0.439
12. 5.000 – 3.299 = 1.701
13. 25/100 = 0.25 = 25%
14. 302/100 = 3.02 = 302%
15. 991/100 = 9.91 = 991%
16. 3/100 = 0.03 = 3%
17. 4/10 = 0.4 = 40%
18. 5/10 = 0.5 = 50%
19. 261.09 = 260 (10s place) 261 (1s place) 261.1 (1/10s place)
20. 5,890,125,837 = 5,890,126,000 (1,000s place) 5,890,100,000 (100,000s place) 5,890,000,000 (1,000,000s place)
21. 2/3 x 2/5 = 4/15
22. 1/7 x 2/3 = 2/21
23. 1/4 x 2/3 = 2/12
24. 3/10 x 2/5 = 6/50
25. 1/4 x 4/7 = 4/28
26. 2/9 x 3/4 = 6/36

Chapter 8 – Day 95

1. Orange
2. Blue
3. Green
4. Purple
5. 4:45 PM
6. 9:15 PM
7. 7:15 PM
8. 10:00 AM
9. 7:15 PM
10. 80 – 45 = 35 ounces
11. 32 – 11 = 21 ounces
12. 1,280 – 384 = 896 ounces
13. 96 – 18 = 78 ounces
14. 128 – 85 = 43 ounces
15. 55 + 60 = 115, 180 – 115 = 65
16. 129 + 20 = 149, 180 – 149 = 31
17. 71 + 38 = 109, 180 – 109 = 71
18. 90 + 25 = 115, 180 – 115 = 65
19. 30 + 115 = 145, 180 – 145 = 35
20. 27 + 85 = 112, 180 – 112 = 68
21. 430 – 30 – 400 years
22. 1155 – 51 = 1,104 years
23. 1820 – 1155 = 665 years
24. 1884 – 826 = 1,058 years
25. 860 – 250 = 610 years
26. 1646 – 600 = 1,046 years

Chapter 8 – Day 96

1. Student to complete, Parent-teacher to check
2. Student to complete, Parent-teacher to check
3. Student to complete, Parent-teacher to check
4. Student to complete, Parent-teacher to check

Chapter 9 – Day 97

a. x (0) + 2 = y (2)
b. x (1) + 2 = y (3)
c. x (2) + 2 = y (4)
d. x (3) + 2 = y (5)
1. $x + 13 = 26, x + 13 - 13 = 26 - 13, x + 0 = 13, x = 13$
2. $x + 15 = 21, x + 15 - 15 = 21 - 15, x + 0 = 6, x = 6$
3. $x + 15 = 30, x + 15 - 15 = 30 - 15, x + 0 = 15, x = 15$
4. $18 + x = 38, 18 + x - 18 = 38 - 18, x + 0 = 20, x = 20$
5. $10 + x = 39, 10 + x - 10 = 39 - 10, x + 0 = 29, x = 29$
6. $39 + x = 43, 39 + x - 39 = 43 - 39, x + 0 = 4, x = 4$
7. 7
8. 10
9. 17
10. 475 ÷ 5 = 95
11. 888 ÷ 4 = 222
12. 277 ÷ 6 = 46 R1
13. 359 ÷ 5 = 71 R4
14. 18 + 23 + 31 + 19 + 11 + 20 + 25 = 147, 147 ÷ 7 = 21 minutes on average per day, 31 – 11 = 20 is the range
15. 21 x 4 = 84, 147 + 84 = 231 total time worked on the puzzle
16. 16 + 14 + 24 + 22 + 17 + 21 = 114, 114 ÷ 6 = 19 weeds pulled on average per morning, 24 – 14 = 10 is the range
17. 19 x 8 = 152, 114 + 152 = 266 total weeds pulled
18. 15 + 8 + 12 + 9 + 11 = 55, 55 ÷ 5 = 11 minutes spent on average per day cleaning your room, 15 – 8 = 7 is the range
19. 7 x 4 = 28, 28 x 11 = 308 minutes spent total on cleaning room every day for 4 weeks
20. 13 + 8 + 14 + 12 + 15 + 9 + 5 + 12 = 88, 88 ÷ 8 = 11 beetles found each day on average, 15 – 5 = 10 is the range
21. 11 x 21 = 231 beetles found in 21 days

Chapter 9 – Day 98

1. $x + 21 = 45, x + 21 - 21 = 45 - 21, x + 0 = 24, x = 24$
2. $x + 9 = 34, x + 9 - 9 = 34 - 9, x + 0 = 25, x = 25$
3. $x + 12 = 26, x + 12 - 12 = 26 - 12, x + 0 = 14, x = 14$
4. $17 + x = 54, 17 + x - 17 = 54 - 17, x = 37$
5. $8 + x = 20, 8 + x - 8 = 20 - 8, x = 12$
6. $14 + x = 47, 14 + x - 14 = 47 - 14, x = 33$
7. 23 x 18 = 414
8. 42 x 14 = 588
9. 34 x 24 = 816
10. 14 x 17 = 238
11. 82 x 11 = 902

12. 33 x 18 = 594
11. 9 5/8
12. 11
13. 4 10/11
14. 4 2/3
15. 7 6/7
16. {3, 6} U {4, 5} = {3, 4, 5, 6}
17. {5, 6} ∩ {3, 6} = {6}
18. {4, 8} U {7, 12} = {4, 7, 8, 12}
19. {3, 7} ∩ {3, 9} = {3}
20. {0, 12} ∩ {0, 12} = {0, 12}
21. {5, 8} U {1, 6} = {1, 5, 6, 8}

Chapter 9 – Day 99

a. y (width of desk) = 7 feet
b. y (width of desk) = 6 feet
c. z (width of room) = 12 feet
1. $3 + y = 10, 3 + y - 3 = 10 - 3, 0 + y = 7, y = 7$
2. $4 + 6 = z, 10 = z$
3. $10 + y = 12, 10 + y - 10 = 12 - 10, 0 + y = 2, y = 2$
4. 3/6 x 2/4 = 6/24
5. 6/24 ÷ 6/6 = 1/4
6. 2/3 x 1/4 = 2/12
7. 2/12 ÷ 2/2 = 1/6
8. 7/8 x 4/5 = 28/40
9. 28/40 ÷ 4/4 = 7/10
10. 4/12 x 1/4 = 4/48
11. 4/48 ÷ 4/4 = 1/12
12. 5/15 x 2/10 = 10/150
13. 10/150 ÷ 10/10 = 1/15
14. (2 x 5) + 4 = 14, 2 4/5 = 14/5
15. (3 x 4) + 3 = 15, 3 3/4 = 15/4
16. (1 x 8) + 7 = 15, 1 7/8 = 15/8
17. (2 x 6) + 5 = 17, 2 5/6 = 17/6
18. 246 ÷ 6 = 41
19. 434 ÷ 7 = 62
20. 686 ÷ 8 = 85 R6

Chapter 9 – Day 100

1. $7 + y = 9, 7 + y - 7 = 9 - 7, 0 + y = 2, y = 2$
2. $11 + y = 12, 11 + y - 11 = 12 - 11, 0 + y = 1, y - 1$
3. $0 + y = 2, y = 2$
4. $125 + y = 200, 125 + y - 125 = 200 - 125, 0 + y = 75, y = 75$
5. $7 + y = 15, 7 + y - 7 = 15 - 7, 0 + y = 8, y = 8$
6. $15 + 85 = z, 100 = z, z = 100$
7. 696 ÷ 8 = 87
8. 673 ÷ 7 = 96 R1
9. 829 ÷ 9 = 92 R1
10. [2, 10)
11. (4, 9]
12. (1, 8)
13. 15 x 14 = 210 sq ft
14. 210 x $9 = $1,890 to hire a carpet installer
15. 210 x $4 = $840 to install carpet yourselves
16. $1,890 – $840 = $1,050 saved by doing it yourself
17. 41 x 37 = 1,517 sq ft
18. 1,517 x $7 = $10,619 to hire a carpet installer
19. 1,517 x $3 = $4,551 to install carpet yourselves
20. $10,619 – $4,551 = $6,068 saved by doing it yourself

Chapter 9 – Day 101

1. x = 85 kilometers, y = distance remaining, z = 185 kilometers, $x + y = z$, $85 + y = 185, 85 + y - 85 = 185 - 85, y + 0 = 100, y = 100$
2. $x = 85$, y = money left, $z = 100, x + y = z, 85 + y = 100, 85 + y - 85 = 100 - 85, y = 15$
3. x = amount spent, $y = 26, x = 80, x + y = z, x + 26 = 80, x + 26 - 26 = 80 - 26, x = 54$
4. $x - 5 = 10$
5. $18 - x = 14$
6. $x \times 3 = 15$
7. $x \div 4 = 4$
8. $20 \div x = 5$
9. 432 ÷ 8 = 54 flowers
10. 32 x 74 = 2,368 milliliters
11. 944 ÷ 4 = 236 miles per day
12. 860 ÷ 5 = 172 milliliters
13. 846 ÷ 6 = 141 cans each
14. 791 ÷ 7 = 113 Bibles in each box
15. 11/15 x 3/3 = 33/45
16. 1/4 x 10/10 = 10/40
17. 4/5 x 9/9 = 36/45
18. 3/9 x 4/4 = 12/36
19. 12/15 ÷ 3/3 = 4/5
20. 3/9 ÷ 3/3 = 1/3
21. 11/33 ÷ 11/11 = 1/3
22. 7/14 ÷ 7/7 = 1/2
23. 255 ÷ 5 = 51
24. 584 ÷ 8 = 73
25. 356 ÷ 7 = 50 R6

Chapter 9 – Day 102

1. t = total number of books, a = number taken away, s = number left, t = unknown, $a = 43, s = 57, t - a = s, t - 43 = 57, t - 43 + 43 = 57 + 43, t - 0 = 100, t = 100$
2. t = total number of marbles, a = number taken away, s = number left, t = unknown, $a = 671, s = 129, t - a = s, t - 671 = 129, t - 671 + 671 = 129 + 671, t - 0 = 800, t = 800$
3. t = total amount of money, a = amount spent, s = amount left, t = unknown, $a = 163, s = 87, t - a = s, t - 163 = 87, t - 163 + 163 = 87 + 163, t - 0 = 250, t = 250$
4. t = total number of pages, a = pages read, s = pages left, t = unknown, $a = 75, s = 40, t - a = s, t - 75 = 40, t - 75 + 75 = 40 + 75, t - 0 = 115, t = 115$
5. t = total number of bulletins, a = bulletins handed out, s = bulletins left, t = unknown, $a = 48, s = 16, t - a = s, t - 48 = 16, t - 48 + 48 = 16 + 48, t - 0 = 64, t = 64$

6. $17 \times 12 = 204$
7. $24 \times 3 = 72$
8. $7 \times 5{,}280 = 36{,}960$
9. $25 \times 4 = 100$
10. $15 \times 16 = 240$
11. $6 \times 128 = 768$
12. $198 \div 9 = 22$
13. $453 \div 2 = 226$ R1
14. $225 \div 6 = 37$ R3
15. $2 \times 365 = 730$
16. $14 \times 60 = 840$
17. $5 \times 52 = 260$
18. $4 \times 24 = 96$
19. $24 \times 60 = 1440$
20. $14 \times 30 = 420$
21. 16: 1, 2, 4, 8, 16
22. 12: 1, 2, 3, 4, 6, 12
23. 4: 1, 2, 4
24. 24: 1, 2, 3, 4, 6, 8, 12, 24

Chapter 9 – Day 103

1. $a \times 9 = 90$, $a \times 9 \div 9 = 90 \div 9$, $a \times 1 = 10$, $a = 10$ rows
2. $6 \times 10 = c$, $6 \times 10 = 60$, $c = 60$ inches
3. $a = 8$ notebooks, $b = 80$ pages, $c =$ unknown total pages, $8 \times 80 = 640$, $c = 640$ total pages
4. $a = 9$ tables, $b = 6$ chairs per table, $c =$ unknown total chairs, $9 \times 6 = 54$, $c = 54$
5. $a =$ unknown number of packs, $b = 5$ pencils per pack, $c = 10$ total pencils, $a \times 5 = 10$, $a \times 5 \div 5 = 10 \div 5$, $a \times 1 = 2$, $a = 2$ packs
6. $a = 3$ cartons, $b =$ unknown amount of eggs per carton, $c = 36$ total eggs, $3 \times b = 36$, $3 \times b \div 3 = 36 \div 3$, $1 \times b = 12$, $b = 12$ eggs per carton
7. $5300 - 2345 = 2955$
8. $5000 - 2345 = 2655$
9. $5000 - 3456 = 1544$
10. 18/40 or 45% are chocolate chip, 22/40 or 55% are sugar
11. 12/30 or 40% are monarchs, 10/30 or 33% are swallowtails, 8/30 or 27% are hairstreaks
12. 15/50 or 30% are oaks, 21/50 or 42% are maples, 14/50 or 28% are pines
13. 2/10 or 20% are sparrows, 3/10 or 30% are robins, 1/10 or 10% are blue jays, 4/10 or 40% are red cardinals
14. 94/100 or 94% sprouted, 6/100 or 6% not sprouted
15. 3/8 or 37.5% are apples, 5/8 or 62.5% are oranges
16. $5/10 < 5/3$
17. $1.7 < 1.8$
18. $0.54 < 0.59$
19. $4/9 > 3/9$
20. $24 \times 26 = 624$
21. $32 \times 19 = 608$
22. $54 \times 29 = 1566$

Chapter 9 – Day 104

1. $a = 6$ jars, $b = 4$ ounces per jar, $6 \times 4 = 24$, $c = 24$
2. $b = 2$ rows, $c = 8$ total plants $a \times 2 = 8$, $a \times 2 \div 2 = 8 \div 2$, $a \times 1 = 4$, $a = 4$
3. $a = 4$ boxes of donuts, $b = 12$ donuts per box, $4 \times 12 = 48$, $c = 48$
4. $a = 8$ bike rides, $c = 24$ total miles, $8 \times b = 24$, $8 \times b \div 8 = 24 \div 8$, $1 \times b = 3$, $b = 3$
5. $a = 5$ chapters per week, $c = 10$ total chapters, $5 \times b = 10$, $5 \times b \div 5 = 10 \div 5$, $1 \times b = 2$, $b = 2$
6. $b = 3$ Sundays, $c = 9$ total tithe, $a \times 3 = 9$, $a \times 3 \div 3 = 9 \div 3$, $a \times 1 = 3$, $a = 3$
7. $8 \times 12 = 96$, $96 + 6 = 102$
8. $2 \times 12 = 24$, $24 + 3 = 27$
9. $49 \times 12 = 588$
10. $5 \times 12 = 60$ inches
11. $8 \times 3 = 24$, $24 + 1 = 25$
12. $4 \times 3 = 12$, $12 + 2 = 14$
13. $12.25 \times 100 = 1{,}225$
14. $22.75 \times 100 = 2{,}275$
15. $17.1 \times 1{,}000 = 17{,}100$
16. $18.25 \times 1000 = 18{,}250$, $18{,}250 \times 100 = 1{,}825{,}000$
17. $x + 17 = 31$, $x + 17 - 17 = 31 - 17$, $x = 14$
18. $x + 5 - 5 = 13 - 5$, $x = 8$
19. $x + 10 = 20$, $x + 10 - 10 = 20 - 10$, $x = 10$
20. $x + 11 = 38$, $x + 11 - 11 = 38 - 11$, $x = 27$

Chapter 9 – Day 105

1. $9 + x = 15$
2. $10 - x = 4$
3. $x - 8 = 2$
4. $5 * x = 30$
5. $x * 6 = 36$
6. $48 \div x = 8$
7. Factors for 12: 1, 2, 3, 4, 6, 12, Factors for 16: 1, 2, 4, 8, 16, GCF: 4
8. $12/16 \div 4/4 = 3/4$
9. Factors for 9: 1, 3, 9, Factors for 15: 1, 3, 5, 15, GCF: 3
10. $9/15 \div 3/3 = 3/5$
11. Factors for 4: 1, 2, 4, Factors for 6: 1, 2, 3, 6, GCF: 2
12. $4/6 \div 2/2 = 2/3$
13. Factors for 5: 1, 5, Factors for 30: 1, 2, 3, 5, 6, 10,15, 30, GCF: 5
14. $5/30 \div 5/5 = 1/6$
15. $24 \times 15 = 360$
16. $32 \times 11 = 352$
17. $39 \times 22 = 858$
18. $15 \times 12 = 180$
19. $71 \times 14 = 994$
20. $24 \times 18 = 432$

Chapter 9 – Day 106

1. $x + 8 = 13$
2. $5 + x = 9$
3. $18 - x = 10$
4. $7 * x = 49$
5. $x \div 9 = 3$
6. $45 \div x = 9$
7. $525 \div 5 = 105$

8. 472 ÷ 8 = 59
9. 929 ÷ 4 = 232 R1
10. $x + 2 - 2 = 17 - 2, x + 0 = 15, x = 15$
11. $x - 3 + 3 = 11 + 3, x - 0 = 14, x = 14$
12. $x \times 4 \div 4 = 8 \div 4, x \times 1 = 2, x = 2$
13. \$20 x 20 = \$400
14. \$20 x 50 = \$1,000
15. \$10 x 30 = \$300
16. \$20 x 14 = \$280
17. \$4 x 120 = \$480
18. \$50,000 x 6 = \$300,000
19. \$960 x 8 = \$7,680
20. 16/18 ÷ 2/2 = 8/9
21. 4/12 ÷ 4/4 = 1/3
22. 12/48 ÷ 12/12 = 1/4

Chapter 9 – Day 107

1. (2, 6)
2. (6, 3)
3. (9, 8)
4. (8, 1)
5. (0, 0)
6. house
7. (4, 3)
8. (2, 5)
9. (1, 8)
10. (7, 9)
11. (9, 2)
12. $7 + y = 9, 7 + y - 7 = 9 - 7, y = 2$
13. $11 + y = 12, 11 + y - 11 = 12 - 11, y = 1$
14. $4 + y = 10, 4 + y - 4 = 10 - 4, y = 6$
15. $6 + y = 13, 6 + y - 6 = 13 - 6, y = 7$
16. $a = 6, c = 600, a \times b = c \rightarrow 6 \times b = 600, 6 \times b \div 6 = 600 \div 6, b \times 1 = 100, b = 100$
17. 1 2/3 → (1 x 3) + 2 = 5 → 5/3
18. 3 3/5 → (3 x 5) + 3 = 18 → 18/5
19. 5 1/4 → (5 x 4) + 1 = 21 → 21/4
20. 8 4/7 → (8 x 7) + 4 = 60 → 60/7
21. 0.9 = 9/10
22. 0.5 = 5/10
23. 0.45 = 45/100
24. 0.96 = 96/100
25. 565 ÷ 5 = 113
26. 308 ÷ 4 = 77
27. 187 ÷ 8 = 23 R3

Chapter 9 – Day 108

N/A – Student to complete, parent-teacher to check

Chapter 10 – Day 109

a. a thousand cubits, ten cubits, thirteen cubits
b. 1,000 x 18 = 18,000, 10 x 18 = 180, 13 x 18 = 234
c. the stars, the wind, the waters
d. God
e. faithful, dishonest
1. Student to complete with parent-teacher's help
2. Student to complete with parent-teacher's help
3. Student to complete with parent-teacher's help
4. $x + 7 = 8, x + 7 - 7 = 8 - 7, x = 1$
5. $x + 3 = 10, x + 3 - 3 = 10 - 3, x = 7$
6. $x + 11 = 22, x + 11 - 11 = 22 - 11, x = 11$
7. $4 + x = 12, 4 + x - 4 = 12 - 4, x = 8$
8. $x + 12 = 34, x + 12 - 12 = 34 - 12, x = 22$
9. $15 + x = 40, 15 + x - 15 = 40 - 15, x = 25$
10. 15 × 12 = 180
11. 62 × 12 = 744
12. 93 × 24 = 2,232
13. 54 × 17 = 918
14. 67 × 63 = 4,221
15. 78 × 28 = 2,184
16. 4 + 7 = 7 + 4 = 11
17. 13 + 16 = 16 + 13 = 29
18. 12 + 27 = 27 + 12 = 39
19. 7 x 5 = 5 x 7 = 35
20. 9 x 7 = 7 x 9 = 63
21. 7 x 10 = 10 x 7 = 70
22. (8 + 4) + 5 = 8 + (4 + 5) = 17
23. (5 + 1) + 9 = 5 + (1 + 9) = 15
24. (6 × 2) × 3 = 6 × (2 × 3) = 36
25. 7 × (3 × 1) = (7 × 3) × 1 = 21

Chapter 10 – Day 110

1. Let x = plants already planted = 4, Let y = more plants you can plant, Let z = total plants = 12, $x + y = z, 4 + y = 12, 4 + y - 4 = 12 - 4, y = 8$
2. Let x = money already saved = 47, Let y = more money needed, Let z = total cost = 125, $x + y = z, 47 + y = 125, 47 + y - 47 = 125 - 47, y = 78$
3. Let x = ounces already filled = 24, Let y = more ounces it can hold, Let z = total ounces = 32, $x + y = z, 24 + y = 32, 24 + y - 24 = 32 - 24, y = 8$
4. Let x = pages already read = 79, Let y = pages left, Let z = total pages = 180, $x + y = z, 79 + y = 180, 79 + y - 79 = 180 - 79, y = 101$
5. Let x = flour already poured = 3, Let y = more flour needed, Let z = total flour = 5, $x + y = z, 3 + y = 5, 3 + y - 3 = 5 - 3, y = 2$
6. Multiplication
7. Subtraction
8. Addition
9. Addition
10. Subtraction
11. Division
12. Division
13. Multiplication
14. Red: 195° Blue: 360° – 195° = 165°
15. Red: 110° Blue: 360° – 110° = 250°
16. Red: 270° Blue: 360° – 270° = 90°
17. Red: 305° Blue: 360° – 305° = 55°

18. Red: 30° Blue: 360° – 30° = 330°
19. Red: 175° Blue: 360° – 175° = 185°

Chapter 10 – Day 111

1. Answers will vary, Parent-teacher to check
2. Answers will vary, Parent-teacher to check
3. Answers will vary, Parent-teacher to check
4. Answers will vary, Parent-teacher to check
5. x + 9 = 18, x + 9 – 9 = 18 – 9, x = 9
6. 44 + x = 55, 44 + x – 44 = 55 – 44, x = 11
7. 26 + x = 40, 26 + x – 26 = 40 – 26, x = 14
8. 300 + x = 450, 300 + x – 300 = 450 – 300, x = 150
9. 2 + x = 8, 2 + x – 2 = 8 – 2, x = 6
10. 80 + x = 150, 80 + x – 80 = 150 – 80, x = 70
11. 792 ÷ 8 = 99
12. 596 ÷ 9 = 66 R2
13. 189 ÷ 3 = 63
14. 475 ÷ 5 = 95
15. 347 ÷ 4 = 86 R3
16. 259 ÷ 6 = 43 R1
17. Factors of 8: 1 × 8 = 8, 2 × 4 = 8, Factors: 1, 2, 4, 8
18. Factors of 9: 1 × 9 = 9, 3 × 3 = 9, Factors: 1, 3, 9
19. Factors of 12: 1 × 12 = 12, 2 × 6 = 12, 3 × 4 = 12, Factors: 1, 2, 3, 4, 6, 12
20. Factors of 31: 1 × 31 = 31, Factors: 1, 31, What do we call a number that only has two factors: A prime number
21. Factors of 18: 1 × 18 = 18, 2 × 9 = 18, 3 × 6 = 18, Factors: 1, 2, 3, 6, 9, 18
22. Factors of 39: 1 × 39 = 39, 3 × 13 = 39, Factors: 1, 3, 13, 39
23. Factors of 16: 1 × 16 = 16, 2 × 8 = 16, 4 × 4 = 16, Factors: 1, 2, 4, 8, 16
24. Factors of 54: 1 × 54 = 54, 2 × 27 = 54, 3 × 18 = 54, 6 × 9 = 54, Factors: 1, 2, 3, 6, 9, 18, 27, 54

Chapter 10 – Day 112

1. 9 + *n* = 15
2. *n* + 6 = 14
3. *N* – 5 = 12
4. 6 x *u* = 36
5. *U* x 4 = 40
6. *U* ÷ 4 = 6
7. 90 – 15 = 75, Complementary
8. 180 – 158 = 22, Supplementary
9. 180 – 41 = 139, Supplementary
10. 90 – 60 = 30, Complementary
11. 90 –72 = 18, Complementary
12. 180 – 25 = 155, Supplementary
13. 0.25 = 25%
14. 1.10 = 110%
15. 0.04 = 4%
16. 0.01 = 1%
17. 0.78 = 78%
18. 1.03 = 103%
19. 3/8 × 4/6 = 12/48
20. Reduce 12/48 ÷ 12/12 = 1/4
21. 3/5 × 5/10 = 15/50
22. Reduce 15/50 ÷ 5/5 = 3/10
23. Numerator = (3 × 5) + 2 = 17, 3 2/5 = 17/5
24. Numerator = (5 × 4) + 1 = 21, 5 1/4 = 21/4
25. Numerator = (6 × 8) + 3 = 51, 6 3/8 = 51/8

Chapter 10 – Day 113

Extra challenge: Student to complete, Parent-teacher to check
1. Equation with numbers: *t* – 9 = 3, Solve: *t* – 9 + 9 = 3 + 9 → *t* = 12
2. Equation with numbers: *t* – 7 = 3, Solve: *t* – 7 + 7 = 3 + 7 → *t* = 10
3. Equation with numbers: *t* – 3 = 2, Solve: *t* – 3 + 3 = 2 + 3 → *t* = 5
4. Answers will vary, parent-teacher to check student's answers. 5 + *x* = 12, *x* = 7
5. Answers will vary, parent-teacher to check student's answers. *x* + 7 = 10, *x* = 3
6. Answers will vary, parent-teacher to check student's answers. 5 – *x* = 3, *x* = 2
7. Answers will vary, parent-teacher to check student's answers. 24 – *x* = 13, *x* = 11
8. 14 x 16 = 224
9. 54 x 9 = 486
10. 92 x 13 = 1,196
11. 85 x 39 = 3,315
12. 73 x 18 = 1,314
13. 54 x 46 = 2,484
14. Answers will vary, Parent-teacher to check
15. Answers will vary, Parent-teacher to check
16. Answers will vary, Parent-teacher to check
17. Answers will vary, Parent-teacher to check
18. 3/3 + 4/3 = 7/3
19. 1/2 – 1/2 = 0
20. 7/8 – 4/8 = 3/8
21. 8/9 + 2/9 = 10/9
22. 3/4 – 2/4 = 1/4
23. 8/10 + 2/10 = 10/10
24. 3/8 + 5/8 = 8/8
25. 5/10 – 2/10 = 3/10
26. 4/6 + 1/6 = 5/6

Chapter 10 – Day 114

1. (0, 5)
2. (2, 3)
3. (7, 1)
4. (9, 8)
5. (5, 6)
6. West
7. West
8. South
9. South
10. South

11. North

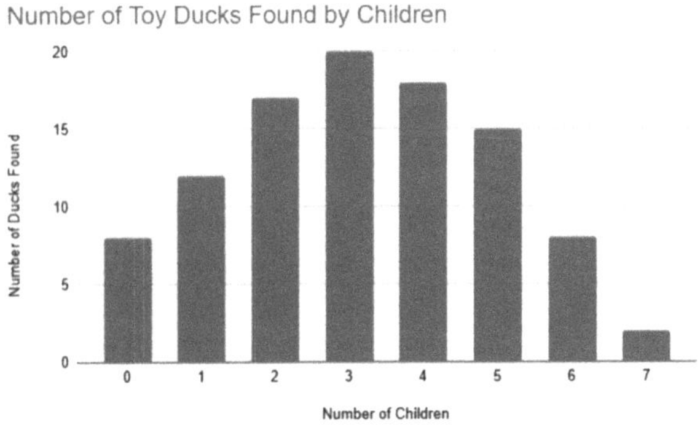

12. 0
13. 7
14. 2 and 4 (answers may vary)
15. 3 (answers may vary)

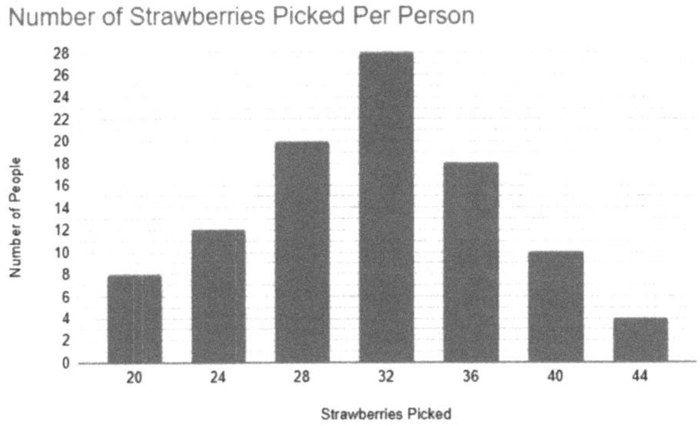

16. 20
17. 44
18. 28 and 36 (answers may vary)
19. 32 (answers may vary)

Chapter 10 – Day 115

1. $a = 16$ (ounces per jar), $b = 8$ (number of jars), $c = ?$ (total ounces), Equation: $16 \times 8 = c$, $c = 128$, Will all the mustard fit into the gallon jar? Yes, Will there be any extra space in the gallon jar? No
2. $a = 2$ (verses to memorize each week), $b = 3$ (number of weeks), $c = 6$ (total verses), Equation: $a \times 3 = 6$, Solve: $a \times 3 \div 3 = 6 \div 3$, $a \times 1 = 2$, $a = 2$
3. $a = 5$ (number of tables), $b = 8$ (chairs per table), $c = 40$ (total chairs), Equation: $5 \times 8 = 40$, $c = 40$
4. $a = 100$ (pieces per box), $b = 4$ (number of boxes), $c = 400$ (total pieces), Equation: $a \times 4 = 400$, Solve: $a \times 4 \div 4 = 400 \div 4 \rightarrow a \times 1 = 100 \rightarrow a = 100$
5. <
6. <
7. >
8. <
9. 3,347, 4,437, 4,743
10. $387 \div 9 = 43$
11. $137 \div 2 = 68$ R1
12. $148 \div 3 = 49$ R1
13. $252 \div 7 = 36$
14. $357 \div 4 = 89$ R1
15. $589 \div 6 = 98$ R1
16. $2{,}000 - 829 = 1{,}171$, $1{,}999 - 828 = 1{,}171$
17. $400 - 74 = 326$, $399 - 73 = 326$
18. $3.859 - 2.579 = 1.28$
19. $6.543 - 2.458 = 4.085$
20. $8.011 - 3.622 = 4.389$

Chapter 10 – Day 116

1. $7 + x = 50$, $7 + x - 7 = 50 - 7$, $x = 43$
2. $t - 35 = 85$, $t - 35 + 35 = 85 + 35$, $t = 120$
3. $400 + x = 950$, $400 + x - 400 = 950 - 400$, $x = 550$
4. $30 - 3 = x$, $30 - 3 = x$, $x = 27$
5. $7 + x = 21$, $7 + x - 7 = 21 - 7$, $x = 14$
6. $4 \times 3 = 12$
7. $21 \div 7 = 3$
8. $3 \times 6 = 18$
9. $24 \div 6 = 4$
10. $70 \div 10 = 7$
11. $4 \times 10 = 40$
12. $25 \div 5 = 5$
13. $10 \times 2 = 20$
14. $2 \times 7 = 14$
15. $51 + 32 = 83$, $180 - 83 = 97$ is the missing angle measurement
16. $90 + 50 = 140$, $180 - 140 = 40$ is the missing angle
17. $22 + 68 = 90$, $180 - 90 = 90$ is the missing angle
18. $55 + 50 = 105$, $180 - 105 = 75$ is the missing angle
19. $65 + 70 = 135$, $180 - 135 = 45$ is the missing angle
20. $15 + 140 = 155$, $180 - 155 = 25$ is the missing angle
21. 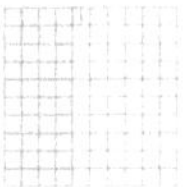
22. 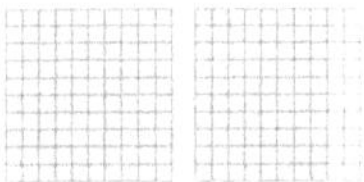
23. 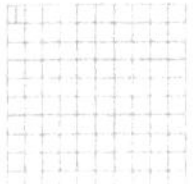
24. 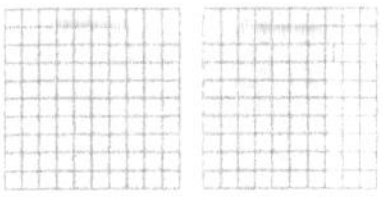
25. 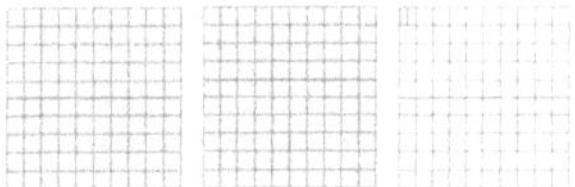
26. 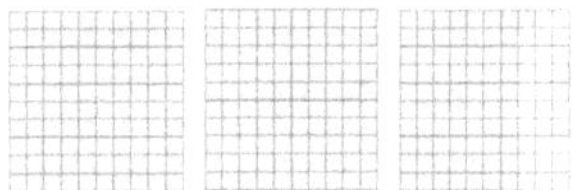
27. $30 - a = 18$, $30 - a + a = 18 + a$, $30 = 18 + a$, $30 - 18 = 18 + a - 18$, $12 = a$

Chapter 10 – Day 117

a. 255 ÷ 5 = 51, 324 ÷ 6 = 54
b. You: 168 ÷ 7 = 24 pages per hour, Friend #1: 216 ÷ 9 = 24 pages per hour, Friend #2: 155 ÷ 5 = 31 pages per hour, Fastest reader: Friend #2
1. 17 + 34 = x, x = 51
2. x + 112 = 451, x + 112 − 112 = 451 − 112, x = 339
3. 2026 − 1776 = x, x = 250
4. t − 17 = 34, t − 17 + 17 = 34 + 17, t = 51
5. 52 × 7 = y, 364 = y
6. y × 4 = 16, y × 4 ÷ 4 = 16 ÷ 4, y × 1 = 4, y = 4
7. 5 x n = 45
8. N ÷ 5 = 7
9. N + 11 = 18
10. 30 − n = 14
11. N x 9 = 72
12. 90 ÷ n = 10
13. 7326 x 7 = 51,282
14. 4982 x 6 = = 29,892
15. 5931 x 9 = 53,379
16. 82 x 23 = 1,886
17. 45 x 15 = 675
18. 63 x 33 = 2,079
19. 7:15pm 
20. 5:30pm 
21. 3:00pm 
22. 9:15am 
23. 10:15am 
24. 8:00am 

Chapter 10 – Day 118

1. 1, 10
2. 2, 0
3. 5, 6
4. 9, 10
5. 6, 3
6. Add 1/3 + 3/4: 1/3 × 4/4 = 4/12, 3/4 × 3/3 = 9/12, 4/12 + 9/12 = 13/12
7. Add 1/2 + 1/4: 1/2 × 4/4 = 4/8, 1/4 × 2/2 = 2/8, 4/8 + 2/8 = 6/8
8. Add 4/5 + 2/3: 4/5 × 3/3 = 12/15, 2/3 × 5/5 = 10/15, 12/15 + 10/15 = 22/15
9. Add 1/4 + 1/6, 1/4 × 6/6 = 6/24, 1/6 × 4/4 = 4/24, 6/24 + 4/24 = 10/24
10. Add 2/5 + 5/9: 2/5 × 9/9 = 18/45, 5/9 × 5/5 = 25/45, 18/45 + 25/45 = 43/45
11. Factors of 4: 1, 2, 4; Factors of 16: 1, 2, 4, 8, 16; Greatest common factor: 4
12. 4/16 ÷ 4/4 = 1/4
13. Factors of 9: 1, 3, 9; Factors of 27: 1, 3, 9, 27; Greatest common factor: 9
14. 9/27 ÷ 9/9 = 1/3
15. Factors of 7: 1, 7; Factors of 21: 1, 3, 7, 21; Greatest common factor: 7 What do we call a number with only two factors? A prime number
16. 7/21 ÷ 7/7 = 1/3
17. Factors of 8: 1, 2, 4, 8; Factors of 18: 1, 2, 3, 6, 9, 18; Greatest common factor: 2
18. 8/18 ÷ 2/2 = 4/9
19. 1 7/9, Numerator = (1 × 9) + 7 = 16, 16/9
20. 3 4/7, Numerator = (3 × 7) + 4 = 25, 25/7
21. 5 3/5, Numerator = (5 × 5) + 3 = 28, 28/5
22. 7 2/3, Numerator = (7 × 3) + 2 = 23, 23/3
23. 5/10 = 0.5
24. 0.1 = 1/10
25. 0.75 = 75/100
26. 2/4 = 0.5

Chapter 10 – Day 119

1. Student to complete, Parent-teacher to check
2. Student to complete, Parent-teacher to check
3. Student to complete, Parent-teacher to check
4. Lily – Gray, Marco – Brown, Noah – Purple, Elena – Orange, Insert filled-in chart
5. Grace – Goldfish, Owen – Hamster, Paul – Dog, Rita – Cat, Insert filled-in chart
6. 25 x 12 = 300
7. 15 x 3 = 45
8. 5280 x 4 = 21,120
9. 13 x 4 = 52
10. 128 x 5 = 640
11. 19 x 16 = 304
12. 504 ÷ 7 = 72
13. 509 ÷ 9 = 56 R5
14. 844 ÷ 4 = 211
15. 295 ÷ 5 = 59
16. 176 ÷ 6 = 29 R2
17. 238 ÷ 3 = 79 R1
18. Let x = exercises already completed, x = 14, Let y = exercises left to do, y = ?, z = 20, Equation: x + y = z, Fill in: 14 + y = 20, 14 + y − 14 = 20 − 14, y = 6
19. t = ?, Let a = number of balloons popped, a = 5, Let s = balloons remaining, s = 24, Equation: t − a = s, Fill in: t − 5 = 24, t − 5 + 5 = 24 + 5, t = 29
20. Let x = pages per notebook, x = 120, Let y = number of notebooks, y = 5, Let z = total pages, z = ?, Equation: x × y = z, Fill in: 120 × 5 = z, z = 600
21. Let x = tracts per person, x = ?, Let y = number of volunteers, y = 9, z = 900, Equation: x × y = z, Fill in: x × 9 = 900, x × 9 ÷ 9 = 900 ÷ 9, x = 100

22. Let x = number of bags, $x = 7$, Let y = pounds per bag, $y = 5$, $z = ?$, Equation: $x \times y = z$, Fill in: $7 \times 5 = z$, $z = 35$
23. Let x = verses per month, $x = ?$, Let y = number of months, $y = 6$, $z = 24$, Equation: $x \times y = z$, Fill in: $x \times 6 = 24$, $x \times 6 \div 6 = 24 \div 6 \rightarrow x = 4$

Chapter 10 – Day 120

N/A – Student to complete, Parent-teacher to check

Chapter 11 – Day 121

a. 20 ÷ 10 = 2
b. 60 ÷ 10 = 6
c. 90 ÷ 10 = 9
d. 25 ÷ 10 = 2 R5
1. 450 ÷ 10 = 45
2. 220 ÷ 10 = 22
3. 355 ÷ 10 = 35 R5
4. 2 1/3 : (3 x 2) + 1 = 7, 2 1/3 = 7/3
5. 3 4/7 : (7 x 3) + 4 = 25, 3 4/7 = 25/7
6. 9 1/8 : (8 x 9) + 1 = 73, 9 1/8 = 73/8
7. 5 5/6 : (6 x 5) + 5 = 35, 5 5/6 = 35/6
8. 2 3/10 : (10 x 2) + 3 = 23, 2 3/10 = 23/10
9. 6 2/3 : (3 x 6) + 2 = 20, 6 2/3 = 20/3
10. 365 x 4 = 1,460 days
11. 60 x 18 = 1,080 minutes
12. 11 x 24 = 264 hours
13. 8 x 7 = 56 days
14. 3/3 + 4/3 = 7/3
15. 1/2 – 1/2 = 0
16. 7/8 – 4/8 = 3/8
17. 8/9 + 2/9 = 10/9
18. 3/4 – 2/4 = 1/4
19. 8/10 + 2/10 = 10/10 = 1
20. 3/8 + 5/8 = 8/8 = 1
21. 5/10 – 2/10 = 3/10

Chapter 11 – Day 122

1. 70 ÷ 10 = 7
2. 830 ÷ 10 = 83
3. 143 ÷ 10 = 14 R3
4. 475 ÷ 10 = 47 R5
5. 800 x 40 = 32,000 (8 x 4 = 32 + 000 = 32,000)
6. 2834 x 9 = 25,506
7. 90 x 30 = 2,700 (9 x 3 = 27 + 00 = 2,700)
8. 4500 x 20 = 90,000 (45 x 2 = 90 + 000 = 90,000)
9. 7026 x 4 = 28,104
10. 2100 x 4000 = 8,400,000 (21 x 4 = 84 + 00000 = 8,400,000)
11. 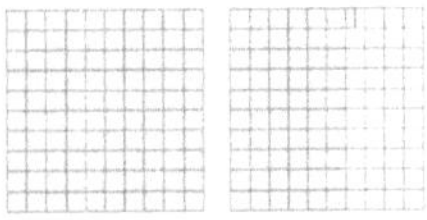
12. 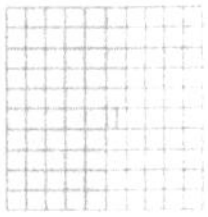
13. 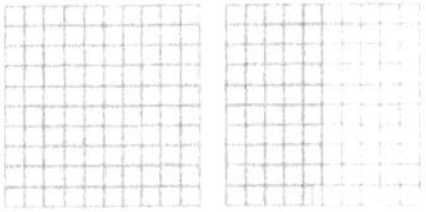
14. 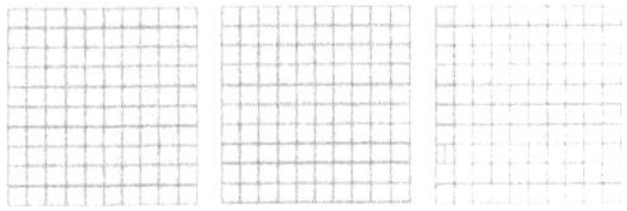
15. 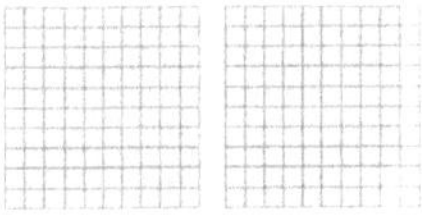
16. 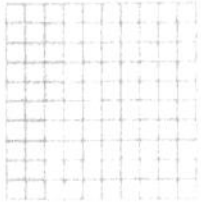
17. $8 + x = 24$, $8 + x - 8 = 24 - 8$, $x = 16$
18. $75 - 8 = x$, $x = 67$
19. $42 + x = 50$, $42 + x - 42 = 50 - 42$, $x = 8$ cups
20. $900 - x = 250$, $900 = 250 + x$, $900 - 250 = 250 + x - 250$, $x = 650$ grams
21. $30 - 12 = x$, $x = 18$ apples
22. $22 + x = 28$, $22 + x - 22 = 28 - 22$, $x = 6$ chapters

Chapter 11 – Day 123

1. 460 ÷ 20 = 23
2. 650 ÷ 50 = 13
3. 450 ÷ 30 = 15
4. 720 ÷ 60 = 12
5. 440 ÷ 40 = 11
6. 840 ÷ 70 = 12
7. 24,573 + 65,324 = 89,897; 89,897 – 65,324 = 24,573
8. 42,159 + 34,820 = 76,979; 76,979 – 34,820 = 42,159
9. 15,447 + 73,052 = 88,499; 88,499 – 73,052 = 15,447
10. 42,375 + 57,314 = 99,689; 99,689 – 57,314 = 42,375
11. $8 + n = 19$
12. $n - 7 = 15$
13. $4 \times n = 40$
14. $N \div 6 = 4$
15. $N \times 6 = 36$
16. $54 \div n = 6$
17 15 x 2.54 = 38.1 centimeters
18. 7 x 1.6 = 11.2 kilometers
19. 5 x 3.8 = 19 liters
20. 12 x 52 = 624 weeks
21. 2 x 30 = 60 days

Chapter 11 – Day 124

1. 428 ÷ 4 = 107

2. 372 ÷ 6 = 62
3. 450 ÷ 10 = 45
4. 589 ÷ 9 = 65 R4
5. 650 ÷ 50 = 13
6. 236 ÷ 3 = 78 R2
7. 32 x 10 = 320
8. 4.67 x 10 = 46.7
9. 17 x 100 = 1,700
10. 15 x 100 = 1,500
11. 5.34 x 10 = 53.4
12. 62.53 x 100 = 6,253
13. 70.6 x 10 = 706
14. 124.2 x 10 = 1,242
15. 209.01 x 10 = 2,090.1
16. 600 – 30 = 570 years
17. 1820 – 51 = 1,769 years
18. 1155 – 860 = 295 years
19. 1884 – 826 = 1,058 years
20. 1870 – 250 = 1,620 years
21. 1646 – 430 = 1,216 years

Chapter 11 – Day 125

1. 744 ÷ 12 = 62
2. 62 x 7 = $434
3. $434 x 9 = $3,906.00
4. 192 ÷ 12 = 16
5. 612 ÷ 12 = 51
6. 264 ÷ 12 = 22
7. 492 ÷ 12 = 41
8. 384 ÷ 12 = 32
9. Answers will vary, parent-teacher to check, $x = 4$
10. Answers will vary, parent-teacher to check, $x = 5$
11. Answers will vary, parent-teacher to check, $x = 7$
12. Answers will vary, parent-teacher to check, $x = 8$
13. 5/6 + 1/2: 5/6 × 2/2 = 10/12, 1/2 × 6/6 = 6/12, 10/12 + 6/12 = 16/12
14. 1/4 + 4/7: 1/4 × 7/7 = 7/28, 4/7 × 4/4 = 16/28, 7/28 + 16/28 = 23/28
15. 7/10 + 2/3: 7/10 × 3/3 = 21/30, 2/3 × 10/10 = 20/30, 21/30 + 20/30 = 41/30
16. 3/9 + 2/3: 3/9 × 3/3 = 9/27, 2/3 × 9/9 = 18/27, 9/27 + 18/27 = 27/27 = 1
17. 1/5 + 1/6: 1/5 × 6/6 = 6/30, 1/6 × 5/5 = 5/30, 6/30 + 5/30 = 11/30
18. 6/7 + 1/9: 6/7 × 9/9 = 54/63, 1/9 × 7/7 = 7/63, 54/63 + 7/63 = 61/63
19. 14: 2, 7 (Answers may vary)
20. 27: 3, 9 (Answers may vary)
21. 16: 2, 8 (Answers may vary)
22. 22: 2, 11 (Answers may vary)
23. 10: 2, 5 (Answers may vary)
24. 12: 3, 4 (Answers may vary)

Chapter 11 – Day 126

1. $x + 4 = 5, x + 4 - 4 = 5 - 4, x = 1$
2. $x + 2 = 10, x + 2 - 2 = 10 - 2, x = 8$
3. $x + 8 = 23, x + 8 - 8 = 23 - 8, x = 15$
4. $10 + x = 23, 10 + x - 10 = 23 - 10, x = 13$
5. $x + 14 = 37, x + 14 - 14 = 37 - 14, x = 23$
6. $23 + x = 48, 23 + x - 23 = 48 - 23, x = 25$
7. 4 + 10 + 7 + 8 + 6 + 9 + 5 = 49, 49 ÷ 7 = 7 ladybugs seen on average per day
8. 10 – 4 = 6 is the range
9. 13 x 49 = 637 ladybugs
10. 15 + 22 + 17 + 20 + 19 + 21 = 114, 114 ÷ 6 = 19 shells collected per day on average
11. 22 – 15 = 7 is the range
12. 18 + 24 + 29 + 21 = 92, 92 ÷ 4 = 23 pinecones collected per day on average
13. 29 – 18 = 11 is the range
14. 23 x 31 = 713 pinecones collected on average for 31 days
15. 65/100, 0.65, 65%
16. 5/100, 0.05, 5%
17. 7/10, 0.7, 70%
18. 7/100, 0.07, 7%

Chapter 11 – Day 127

1. 750 ÷ 30 = 25
2. 132 ÷ 11 = 12
3. 583 ÷ 11 = 53
4. 572 ÷ 11 = 52
5. 451 ÷ 11 = 41
6. 693 ÷ 11 = 63
7. (3, 8)
8. (7, 5)
9. (1, 1)
10. (4, 10)
11. (9, 9)
12. 2 1/4 + 1/4 + 3 2/4 = 6
13. 2 1/2 + 3 1/2 = 6
14. 4 2/9 + 1 5/9 = 5 7/9
15. 4 2/3 + 3 2/3 = 8 1/3
16. 1/9 + 3 1/9 + 1 + 2 2/9 = 6 4/9
17. 1 1/7 + 2 5/7 + 4 4/7 + 2 6/7 = 11 2/7
18. 2 3/8 : (8 × 2) + 3 = 19, 19/8
19. 4 5/7 : (7 × 4) + 5 = 33, 33/7
20. 6 1/6 : (6 × 6) + 1 = 37, 37/6
22. 8 2/3 : (3 × 8) + 2 = 26, 26/3
23. 7/10 = 0.7
24. 0.3 = 3/10
25. 0.85 = 85/100
26. 4/8 = 0.5

Chapter 11 – Day 128

1. 8 x 12 = 96
2. 96 + 3 = 99 inches
3. 25 x 12 = 300 inches
4. 6 x 12 = 72
5. 72 + 9 = 81 inches
6. 47 x 12 = 564 inches

7. 4 x 3 = 12
8. 12 + 2 = 14 feet
9. 35 x 3 = 105 feet
10. 440 ÷ 20 = 22
11. 780 ÷ 60 = 13
12. 671 ÷ 11 = 61
13. 341 ÷ 11 = 31
14. 372 ÷ 12 = 31
15. 768 ÷ 12 = 64
16. 9.05 x 100 = 905cm
17. 13.25 x 1,000 = 13,250m
18. 2.6042 x 1,000 = 2,604.2m
19. 2,604.2 x 100 = 260,420cm
20. <
21. <
22. >
23. <
24. {1, 2, 4, 9}
25. {1, 5, 6, 8}
26. None
27. {10}
28. {0}
29. {3, 6, 7}

Chapter 11 – Day 129

a. 12 x 32 = 384
b. $384 x 7 = $2,688.00
1. 15 x 1 = 15, 15 x 2 = 30, 15 x 3 = 45, 15 x 4 = 60, 495 ÷ ÷ 15 = 33
2. 16 x 1 = 16, 16 x 2 = 32, 16 x 3 = 48, 16 x 4 = 64, 384 ÷ 16 = 24
3. 17 x 1 = 17, 17 x 2 = 34, 17 x 3 = 51, 17 x 4 = 68, 697 ÷ 17 = 41
4. $20 x 17 = $340.00
5. 85 x $4 = $340.00
6. $50,000 x 12 = $600,000.00
7. $960 x 9 = $8,640.00
8. (2 x 3) + 1 = 7, 3 1/2 = 7/2
9. 7/2 x 1/7 = 7/14
10. 7/14 ÷ 7/7 = 1/2
11. (5 x 3) + 4 = 19, 3 4/5 = 19/5
12. 19/5 x 1/4 = 19/20
13. Multiplication
14. Subtraction
15. Addition
16. Division
17. Subtraction
18. Division
19. Division
20. Multiplication

Chapter 11 – Day 130

1. 12/30 or 40% were blueberry, 18/30 or 60% were banana nut
2. 10/25 or 40% were sparrows, 9/25 or 36% were robins, 6/25 or 24% were cardinals
3. 16/40 or 40% were bluegill, 14/40 or 35% were bass, 10/40 or 25% were catfish
4. 9/20 or 45% were ants, 4/20 or 20% were beetles, 7/20 or 35% were grasshoppers
5. 18/45 or 40% were tan, 12/45 or 27% were black, 5/45 or 11% were red, 10/45 or 22% were silver
6. 8/15 or 53% were mallards, 7/15 or 47% were wood ducks
7. 3/8 × 4/4 = 12/32
8. 4/9 × 2/2 = 8/18
9. 22/55 ÷ 11/11 = 2/5
10. 14/70 ÷ 7/7 = 2/10
11. 6/7 × 7/7 = 42/49
12. 9/11 × 5/5 = 45/55
13. 9/81 ÷ 9/9 = 1/9
14. 12/54 ÷ 6/6 = 2/9
15.

	A	B
1	Person	Fish Caught
2	Matthew	1
3	Mark	4
4	Luke	3
5	John	7
6	Peter	10
7	Sum	=SUM(B2:B6)
8	Average	=AVERAGE(B2:B6)
9	Range	=MAX(B2:B6)–MIN(B2:B6)

16.

	A	B
1	Person	Minutes Walked
2	Alex	24
3	Jordan	32
4	Chris	28
5	Morgan	35
6	Noah	22
7	Jose	27
8	Sum	=SUM(B2:B7)
9	Average	=AVERAGE(B2:B7)
10	Range	=MAX(B2:B7)–MIN(B2:B7)

17.

	A	B
1	Animal	Sold
2	Fish	28
3	Hamsters	12
4	Birds	9
5	Dogs	10
6	Lizards	5
7	Sum	=SUM(B2:B6)
8	Average	=AVERAGE(B2:B6)
9	Range	=MAX(B2:B6)–MIN(B2:B6)

Chapter 11 – Day 131

a. 1 x 30 = 30, 2 x 30 = 60, 3 x 30 = 90, 750 ÷ 30 = 25
1. 51 ÷ 3 = 17 yards
2. 192 ÷ 16 = 12 pounds
3. 540 ÷ 30 = 18 feet
4. 98 ÷ 3 = 32 yards R2
5. 129 ÷ 3 = 43 yards
6. 516 ÷ 12 = 43 feet
7. 672 ÷ 12 = 56 feet
8. 384 ÷ 12 = 32 feet

9. 3000 – 473 = 2,527, 2999 – 472 = 2,527
10. 600 – 367 = 233, 599 – 366 = 233
11. 1000 – 925 = 75, 999 – 924 = 75
12. 2000 – 548 = 1,452, 1999 – 547 = 1,452
13. 11 x 5 = 55, 11 x 6 = 66, 11 x 7 = 77, 11 x 8 = 88, 792 ÷ 11 = 72
14. 15 x 1 = 15, 15 x 2 = 30, 15 x 3 = 45, 15 x 4 = 60, 485 ÷ 15 = 32 R5
15. 16 x 1 = 16, 16 x 2 = 32, 16 x 3 = 48, 16 x 4 = 64, 368 ÷ 16 = 23
16. 17x 1 = 17, 17 x 2 = 34, 17 x 3 = 51, 17 x 4 = 68, 697 ÷ 17 = 41
17. 18 x 1 = 18, 18 x 2 = 36, 18 x 3 = 54, 18 x 4 = 72, 594 ÷ 18 = 33
18. 8/20
19. 3/20
20. 5/20
21. 4/20
22. 11/20
23. 9/20
24. 16 x 2 = 32, 16 x 3 = 48, 16 x 4 = 64, 16 x 5 = 80, 16 x 6 = 96, 96 ÷ 16 = 6 pounds
25. 336 ÷ 16 = 21 pounds
26. 396 ÷ 12 = 33 feet

Chapter 11 – Day 132

1. Student to complete, Parent-teacher to check
2. Student to complete, Parent-teacher to check

Chapter 12 – Day 133

a. 20 + 24 + 23 + 25 + 21 = 113, 113 ÷ 5 = 22 R3
b. 18 + 19 + 21 + 24 + 23 = 105, 105 ÷ 5 = 21
c. 17 + 15 + 20 + 15 + 16 = 83, 83 ÷ 5 = 16 R3
d. Chemical C would be the best option for helping ice melt on sidewalks.
Activity: Student to complete, Parent-teacher to check
1. Answers will vary, Parent-teacher to check
2. Answers will vary, Parent-teacher to check
3. Answers will vary, Parent-teacher to check
4. Answers will vary, Parent-teacher to check
5. Answers will vary, Parent-teacher to check
6. Answers will vary, Parent-teacher to check
7. 5 + 7 = 7 + 5 = 12
8. 14 + 23 = 23 + 14 = 37
9. 48 + 57 = 57 + 48 = 105
10. 4 × 5 = 5 × 4 = 20
11. 3 × 8 = 8 × 3 = 24
12. 7 × 11 = 11 × 7 = 77
13. Factors of 10: 1, 2, 5, 10
14. Factors of 16: 1, 2, 4, 8, 16
15. Factors of 22: 1, 2, 11, 22
16. Factors of 32: 1, 2, 4, 8, 16, 32
17. Factors of 25: 1, 5, 25
18. 3:15PM 
19. 12:00PM 
20. 3:15PM 
21. 6:15PM 
22. 5:15PM 
23. 3:00PM 

Chapter 12 – Day 134

1. 82 + 95 + 88 + 91 + 84 = 440
2. 440 ÷ 5 = 88 seconds
3. 55 + 48 + 52 + 49 + 46 = 250
4. 250 ÷ 5 = 50 seconds
5. 18 + 22 + 19 + 21 + 20 = 100
6. 100 ÷ 5 = 20 seconds, The hot water dissolved the salt the fastest
7. To get the most consistent, accurate results, everything must be the same and even as possible.
8. 54179 + 43120 = 97299; 97299 – 43120 = 54179
9. 44728 + 14061 = 58789; 58789 – 14061 = 44728
10. 35463 + 63202 = 98665; 98665 – 63202 = 35463
11. 12475 + 37514 = 49989; 49989 – 37514 = 12475
12. 33671 + 43101 = 76772; 76772 – 43101 = 33671
13. 49175 + 50804 = 99979; 99979 – 50804 = 49175
14. 3/12 + 3/6 = 3/12 + 6/12 = 9/12
15. 1/12 + 1/4 = 1/12 + 3/12 = 4/12
16. 1/4 + 2/8 = 2/8 + 2/8 = 4/8
17. 3/4 + 3/12 = 9/12 + 3/12 = 12/12
18. 12/12 – 5/6 = 12/12 – 10/12 = 2/12
19. 4/8 – 3/6 = 4/8 – 4/8 = 0/8
20. 11/12 – 5/6 = 11/12 – 10/12 = 1/12
21. 7/8 – 1/4 = 7/8 – 2/8 = ⅝
22. 176 ÷ 11 = 16
23. 345 ÷ 15 = 23
24. 180 ÷ 12 = 15
25. 357 ÷ 17 = 21

Chapter 12 – Day 135

a. Student to complete, Parent-teacher to check
b. Student to complete, Parent-teacher to check
1. 75x68 = 5,100

2. 58x44 = 2,552
3. 85x71 = 6,035
4. 97x42 = 4,074
5. 99x33 = 3,267
6. 81x13 = 1,053
7. Factors of 23: 1 × 23 = 23; Factors: 1, 23; A number with only two factors is called a prime number
8. Factors of 26: 1 × 26 = 26 | 2 × 13 = 26; Factors: 1, 2, 13, 26
9. Factors of 28: 1 × 28 = 28 | 2 × 14 = 28 | 4 × 7 = 28; Factors: 1, 2, 4, 7, 14, 28
10. Factors of 48: 1 × 48 = 48 | 2 × 24 = 48 | 3 × 16 = 48 | 4 × 12 = 48 | 6 × 8 = 48; Factors: 1, 2, 3, 4, 6, 8, 12, 16, 24, 48
11. 6/8 ÷ 2/2 = 3/4
12. 8/16 ÷ 4/4 = 2/4
13. 8/10 ÷ 2/2 = 4/5
14. 15/25 ÷ 5/5 = 3/5
15. 6/9 ÷ 3/3 = 2/3
16. 44/77 ÷ 11/11 = 4/7

Chapter 12 – Day 136

1. Answers will vary, Parent-teacher to check
2. Answers will vary, Parent-teacher to check
3. 10.3 + 9.7 + 10.2 + 9.8 + 12.0 = 52
4. 52 ÷ 5 = 10 R2 (10.4)
5. 10.6 + 10.4 + 10.9 + 10.7 + 10.4 = 53
6. 53 ÷ 5 = 10 R3 (10.6)
7. Answers will vary, Parent-teacher to check
8. He could have tripped
9. Using the average is a fairer way to compare because something could go wrong in just one try, and using the average will make it more even.
10. Answers will vary
11. 135°
12. 360°– 135° = 225°
13. Answers will vary
14. 225°
15. 360° – 225° = 135°
16. Answers will vary
17. 210°
18. 360° – 210° = 150°
19. Answers will vary
20. 150°
21. 360°– 150° = 210°
22. 180 – 43 = 137, Supplementary
23. 180 – 90 = 90, Supplementary
24. 90 – 50 = 40, Complementary
25. 90 – 25 = 65, Complementary
26. 90 – 45 = 45, Complementary
27. 180 – 151 = 29, Supplementary

Chapter 12 – Day 137

Activity: Student to complete, Parent-teacher to check
1. 4/5 × 3/6 = 12/30
2. Reduce: 12/30 ÷ 6/6 = 2/5
3. 3/4 × 8/10 = 24/40
4. Reduce: 24/40 ÷ 8/8 = 3/5
5. 6/9 × 2/3 = 12/27
6. Reduce: 12/27 ÷ 3/3 = 4/9
7. 2/5 × 10/6 = 20/30
8. Reduce: 20/30 ÷ 10/10 = 2/3
9. 1/2 × 6/5 = 6/10
10. Reduce: 6/10 ÷ 2/2 = 3/5
11. 6/8 × 2/8 = 12/64
12. Reduce: 12/64 ÷ 4/4 = 3/16
13. 2 1/2 – 1 1/2 = 1
14. 2 2/4 + 3/4 + 1 2/4 = 4 3/4
15. 7 3/10 + 1 8/10 = 9 1/10
16. 7 6/9 – 2 4/9 – 1 1/9 = 4 1/9
17. 1 1/3 + 2 2/3 + 4 1/3 = 8 1/3
18. 4/5 + 3 2/5 + 1 + 2 3/5 = 7 4/5

Chapter 12 – Day 138

1. 20 + 25 + 25 + 30 + 25 = 125
2. 125 ÷ 5 = 25 minutes on average for the water to dry in front of of the fan
3. 50 + 50 + 45 + 55 + 50 = 250
4. 250 ÷ 5 = 50 minutes on average for the water to dry in front of of the fan
5. 30 – 20 = 10 is the range
6. 55 – 45 = 10 is the range
7. The water in front of the fan evaporated faster
8. It is important to use the same amount of water and plate for the experiments so you get the most accurate result.
9. The water in front of the fan evaporated twice as fast as the water not in air flow.
10. Answers will vary – Potentially, if the fan was on double the speed, it could dry twice as fast.
11. Answers will vary, Parent-teacher to check
12. Answers will vary, Parent-teacher to check
13. Answers will vary, Parent-teacher to check
14. Answers will vary, Parent-teacher to check
15. 40 ÷ 2.5 = 16
16. 35 x 2.2 = 77
17. 18 ÷ 2.2 = 8.18
18. 12 x 1.6 = 19.2
19. 15 x 3.8 = 57
20. 45 ÷ 1.6 = 28.125
21. 0.77 = 77%
22. 1.60 = 160%
23. 2.50 = 250%
24. 0.08 = 8%
25. 0.45 = 45%
26. 1.02 = 102%

Chapter 12 – Day 139

a. 551 ÷ 12 = 45 R11
b. 610 ÷ 12 = 50 R10
c. 671 ÷ 12 = 55 R11

d. 732 ÷ 12 = 61 R0
1. 6000 x 50 = 300,000 (6 x 5 = 30 + 0000 = 30,000)
2. 490 x 60 = 29,400 (49 x 6 = 294 + 00 = 29,400)
3. 5870 x 7 = 41,090 (587 x 7 = 4,109 + 0 = 41,090)
4. 361 x 40 = 14,440 (361 x 4 = 1,444 + 0 = 14,440)
5. 8,400 x 20 = 168,000 (84 x 2 = 168 + 000 = 168,000)
6. 450 x 120 = 54,000 (45 x 12 = 540 + 00 = 54,000)
7. 4/5 × 5/5 = 20/25
8. 3/11 × 3/3 = 9/33
9. 30/45 ÷ 15/15 = 2/3
10. 32/64 ÷ 16/16 = 2/4
11. 8/12 × 4/4 = 32/48
12. 1/15 × 2/2 = 2/30
13. 34/51 ÷ 17/17 = 2/3
14. 54/72 ÷ 18/18 = 3/4
15. 3/5 + 3/4 → 3/5 × 4/4 = 12/20 → 3/4 × 5/5 = 15/20 → 12/20 + 15/20 = 27/20
16. 5/8 + 4/7 → 5/8 × 7/7 = 35/56 → 4/7 × 8/8 = 32/56 → 35/56 + 32/56 = 67/56
17. 4/11 + 2/3 → 4/11 × 3/3 = 12/33 → 2/3 × 11/11 = 22/33 → 12/33 + 22/33 = 34/33
18. 2/9 + 5/6 → 2/9 × 6/6 = 12/54 → 5/6 × 9/9 = 45/54 → 12/54 + 45/54 = 57/54
19. 10/12 + 1/6 → 10/12 x 6/6 = 60/72 → 1/6 x 12/12 = 12/72 → 60/72 + 12/72 = 72/72

Chapter 12 – Day 140

1. 115 + 120 + 110 + 125 + 118 + 122 + 120 + 116 + 124 + 130 = 1,200, 1,200 ÷ 10 = 120 minute average battery life for brand 1
2. 145 + 150 + 140 + 155 + 148 + 152 + 150 + 146 + 154 + 160 = 1,500, 1,500 ÷ 10 = 150 minute average battery life for brand 2
3. 175 + 180 + 170 + 185 + 178 + 182 + 180 + 176 + 184 + 190 = 1,800, 1,800 ÷ 10 = 180 minute average battery life for brand 3
4. No, it would not be worth it to buy brand 1 if it was twice as much because it does not produce twice the amount of energy.
5. 585 ÷ 13 = 45
6. 589 ÷ 9 = 65 R4
7. 210 ÷ 15 = 14
8. 672 ÷ 12 = 56
9. 599 ÷ 8 = 74 R7
10. 272 ÷ 17 = 16
11. 40 x 12 = 480 months
12. 52 ÷ 7 = 7 R3 weeks
13. 24 x 4 = 96 hours
14. 52 x 20 = 1,040 weeks
15. 24 x 3 = 72 hours, 72 x 60 = 4,320 minutes
16. 51 + 39 = 90, 180 – 90 = 90 is the missing angle measurement
17. 33 + 90 = 123, 180 – 123 = 57 is the missing angle measurement
18. 104 + 33 = 137, 180 – 137 = 43 is the missing angle measurement
19. 21 + 132 = 153, 180 – 153 = 27 is the missing angle measurement
20. 60 + 60 = 120, 180 – 120 = 60 is the missing angle measurement
21. 28 + 83 = 111, 180 – 111 = 69 is the missing angle measurement

Chapter 12 – Day 141

1. $10 + $15 + $14 + $14 + $12 = $65.00, 65 ÷ 5 = $13 made on average for week 1
2. $15 + $13 + $14 + $15 + $13 = $70.00, 70 ÷ 5 = $14 made on average for week 2
3. $15 + $15 + $14 + $13 + $13 = $70.00, 70 ÷ 5 = $14 made on average for week 3
4. $13 + $15 + $14 + $16 + $17 = $75.00, 75 ÷ 5 = $15 made on average for week 4
5. $14 + $18 + $17 + $15 + $16 = $80.00, 80 ÷ 5 = $16 made on average for week 5
6.

7. (2, 2)
8. (4, 9)
9. (6, 1)
10. (0, 10)
11. (9, 5)
12. 14/15 or 93% are sheep, 1/15 or 7% are cows.
13. 15/27 or 56% are pigeons, 7/27 or 26% are mockingbirds, 5/27 or 18% are sparrows.
14. 59/100 or 59% are striped bass, 34/100 or 34% are rainbow trout, 7/100 or 7% are catfish.
15. 28/70 or 40% are pennies, 17/70 or 24% are nickels, 10/70 or 14% are dimes, 15/70 or 22% are quarters.
16. 40/80 or 50% are peanuts, 18/80 or 23% are raisins, 14/80 or 17% are almond, 8/80 or 10% are chocolate chips
17. 2/12 or 17% good report, 10/12 or 83% bad report.
18. 75/100, 0.75, 75%
19. 23/100, 0.23, 23%
20. 41/100, 0.41, 41%
21. 4/10, 0.4, 40%
22. 3 5/6: (3 × 6) + 5 = 23/6
23. 4 7/9: (4 × 9) + 7 = 43/9
24. 2 4/5: (2 × 5) + 4 = 14/5
25. 7 2/3: (7 × 3) + 2 = 23/3
26. 2 9/10: (2 × 10) + 9 = 29/10
27. 2 13/15: (2 × 15) + 13 = 43/15

Chapter 12 – Day 142

1. 3 + 5 + 4 + 2 + 6 = 20, 20 ÷ 5 = 4 cm on average for week 1
2. 9 + 11 + 10 + 8 + 12 = 50, 50 ÷ 5 = 10 cm on average for week 2
3. 16 + 18 + 17 + 15 + 19 = 85, 85 ÷ 5 = 17 cm on average for week 3

4. 23 + 24 + 22 + 21 + 25 = 115, 115 ÷ 5 = 23 cm on average for week 4

5.

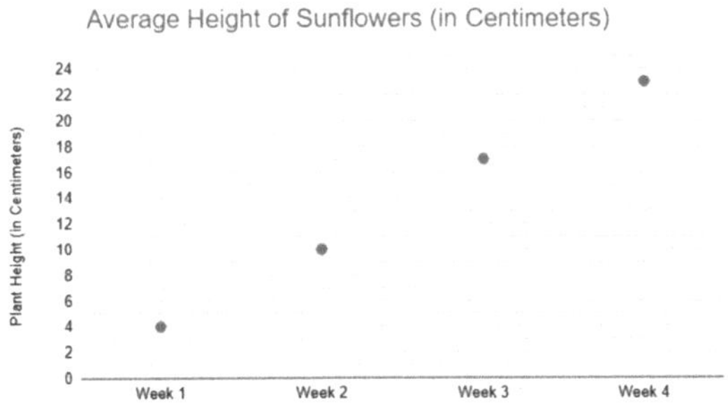

6. 3 × 12 = 36, 36 + 6 = 42 inches
7. 5 × 12 = 60, 60 + 9 = 69 inches
8. 37 × 12 = 444 inches
9. 23 × 12 = 276 inches
10. 4 × 3 = 12, 12 + 2 = 14 feet
11. 31 × 3 = 93 feet
12. 9.42 × 100 = 942 cm
13. 25.3 × 1,000 = 25,300 m
14. 10.07 × 100 = 1,007 cm
15. $x + 5 = 12, x + 5 - 5 = 12 - 5, x = 7$
16. $x + 8 = 21, x + 8 - 8 = 21 - 8, x = 13$
17. $x + 0 = 8, x = 8$
18. $11 + x = 33, 11 + x - 11 = 33 - 11, x = 22$
19. Answers will vary, 300°
20. Answers will vary, 150°
21. Answers will vary, 60°
22. Answers will vary, 330°

Chapter 12 – Day 143

1. 520 ÷ 13 = 40
2. 674 ÷ 7 = 96 R2
3. 945 ÷ 15 = 63
4. 594 ÷ 18 = 33
5. 389 ÷ 6 = 64 R5
6. 832 ÷ 16 = 52
7. \$20 x 34 = \$680.00
8. \$4 x 74 = \$296.00
9. \$50,000 x 5 = \$250,000.00
10. \$960 x 3 = \$2,880.00
11. $N + 9 = 21$
12. $15 - N = 8$
13. $N + 7 = 17$
14. $3 \times N = 18$
15. $N \div 9 = 3$
16. $70 \div N = 7$
17. Answers will vary, 3 + 4 = 7
18. Answers will vary, 8 + 1 = 9
19. Answers will vary, 10 – 10 = 0
20. Answers will vary, 24 – 12 = 12
21. Eric: blue, Faith: green, Greg: red, Holly: yellow
22. Mike: brown, Noah: grey, James: orange, Pam: green

Chapter 12 – Day 144

1. Answers will vary, Student to complete, Parent-teacher to check
2. Answers will vary, Student to complete, Parent-teacher to check
3. Answers will vary, Student to complete, Parent-teacher to check
4. Answers will vary, Student to complete, Parent-teacher to check